3 Plays

by Ed Schmidt

Books We Live by - New York

3 Plays © 2025 by Ed Schmidt

Library of Congress Catalog Card Number:

ISBN: Trade 978-1-62848-070-2

ISBN: MOBI 978-1-62848-068-9

ISBN: EPUB 978-1-62848-069-6

Published by Books We Live by, NY

360 West 118th Street, New York, NY, 10026

www.BooksWeLiveBy.com

First edition. All rights reserved, including English and all foreign languages and media. This book may not be used or reproduced, in whole or in part, including illustrations, in any form (beyond that copying permitted by Sections 107 and 108 of the U.S. Copyright Law and except by reviewers for the public press), without written permission from the publisher.

Caution: professionals and amateurs are hereby warned that all materials in this book, being fully protected under the copyright laws of the United States of America, the British Empire, including the Dominion of Canada, and all other countries of the Berne and Universal Copyright Convention, is subject to royalty. All rights, including professional, amateur, motion picture, recitation, lecturing, public reading, radio and television broadcasting, and the rights of translations into foreign languages, are strictly reserved. The rights for this edition are controlled exclusively by Books We Live by. Inquiries concerning all the rights delineated above should be addressed to Books We Live by, New York.

This play collection contains: *The Last Supper* © Ed Schmidt 2001
My Last Play © Ed Schmidt 2010
Our Last Game © Ed Schmidt 2015

Cover Design: Sophie Blackall

File under: Theater / Performance Arts

Manufactured in the United States of America 10 9 8 7 6 5 4 3 2 1

Acknowledgments

Arnold Barkus, Sophie Blackall, Mary Bolster, Tom Bolster, J. Nicole Brooks, Rob Campbell, Tisa Chang, Frederic Colier, Erin Craig, Bill Craver, Jed Distler, Sheldon Epps, Carol Fineman, Howard Fishman, Eggy Godlee, Olive Godlee, Hugh Hayes, David Hill, Mary Beth Kilkelly, Beatrice Kilkelly-Schmidt, Jack Kilkelly-Schmidt, Todd Lubin, Marti Lyons, B. Rodney Marriott, Ethan McSweeny, Jack O'Brien, Jack Parsons, Vicky Raab, Jeffrey Richards, Lois Schmidt, Steve Schmidt, Willie Schmidt, Max Shuppert, Gregg Thomas, Chris Till, Henry Timm, Bruce Weber, Alan Wilkinson, Caveh Zahedi, and Jeff Zinn.

Table of Contents

Acknowledgments
The Last Supper .... p 1
My Last Play .... p 47
Our Last Game .... p 105
About the Author
About Books We Live by

THE LAST SUPPER

(a Comedy)

Cast & Productions

The Last Supper opened in April 2002, at 410 16th Street, Brooklyn, New York.

The play moved to 124 West 27th Street, Apartment 4W, New York City, on October 17, 2003.

The play was performed at the Bonn Biennale, in Bonn, Germany, in June 2004.

The play was again performed at the Philadelphia Live Arts Festival, in September 2004.

The play was performed for the final time at Monroe Denton's apartment in Williamsburg, Brooklyn, on April 16 and 17, 2016.

In all productions, Ed Schmidt played the role of ED SCHMIDT.

3 Plays

THE LAST SUPPER

(a Comedy)

Time: *Now*

Place: ED SCHMIDT's *kitchen, dining room, and living room.*

In the kitchen, two long church pews. Six hymnals on each pew. Along the back wall: a stainless-steel countertop; birch-veneer cabinets from IKEA; shelves containing cookbooks, a dictionary, a Complete Works of William Shakespeare, and a few other plays. A refrigerator, stove, sink, dishwasher, microwave.

A clock on a side wall.

Magnetted to the refrigerator: family photos, kids' drawings, a minister's certificate, a typed letter to the IRS. On the countertop, among the usual kitchen stuff: a child's Easter basket, a child's fireman's helmet.

An island with a butcher-block countertop stands between the pews and the cooking area. On the island: a Bible, a glass of water, a cellphone, an unbound copy of the script for "The Last Supper," a chef's knife, a cutting board, etc. A stool next to the island.

A red velvet curtain, undrawn at the top of the show, separates the kitchen from the dining room. A bare dining table large enough to accommodate fifteen people. No tablecloth, no plates or glasses or silverware. A chandelier with unlit candles.

Beyond the dining room is the living room. A couch, some chairs, bookshelves. The usual.

As the audience enters through the back door and sits in the pews, ED SCHMIDT *comes in and out of the kitchen. He putters around, checks a few props, perhaps says hello to an audience member or two. He seems mildly distracted, mildly flustered.*

This play is fully scripted, but the audience should suspect much of it is not.

Ed Schmidt

After everyone is seated, ED SCHMIDT *draws the red curtain closed, steps behind the island and addresses the audience.*

ED SCHMIDT

Please turn in your hymnals to hymn number 47, "I Love to Tell the Story." We will stand and sing the first verse only.

> *The audience stands. He leads them in singing the first verse of "I Love to Tell the Story."*

"I love to tell the story

Of unseen things above,

Of Jesus and his glory,

Of Jesus and his love.

I love to tell the story,

Because I know it's true;

It satisfies my longings

As nothing else can do.

I love to tell the story,

'Twill be my theme in glory,

To tell the old, old story

Of Jesus and his love."

> *The audience sits. He opens a Bible.*

A reading from the holy gospel according to St. John. "And Jesus went up into a mountain, and there he sat with his disciples. And the Passover, a feast of the Jews, was nigh. When Jesus then lifted up his eyes, and saw a great company come unto him, he saith unto Philip, 'Whence shall we buy bread, that these may eat?' And this he said to prove him, for he himself knew what he would do. Philip answered him, 'Two hundred pennyworth of bread is not sufficient for them, that every one of them may take a little.' One of his disciples, Andrew, Simon Peter's brother, saith unto him, 'There is a lad here, which hath five barley loaves and two small fishes, but what are they among so many?' And Jesus said, 'Make the men sit down.' Now there was much grass in the place. So the men sat down, in number about five thousand. And Jesus took the loaves, and when he had given thanks, he distributed to the disciples, and the disciples to them that were set down, and likewise of the fishes as much as they would. When they were filled, he said unto his disciples, 'Gather up the fragments that remain, that nothing be lost.' Therefore they gathered them together, and filled twelve baskets with the fragments of the five barley loaves, which remained over and above unto them that had eaten. Then those men, when they had seen the miracle that Jesus did, said, 'This is of a truth that Prophet that should come into the world.'" This is the word of the Lord. Five loaves of bread, two fishe— two *small* fishes, five thousand people. Jesus, with five loaves of bread and two small fishes, fed five thousand people. And not only did Jesus feed five thousand with five loaves of bread and two small fishes, he fed them until they were full. And not only did he feed them until they were full, but there were leftovers. And not only were there leftovers, but from five loaves of bread there were twelve baskets of leftovers. The leftovers exceeded, by more than double, the original amount. This is the miracle of the loaves and the fishes.

Conspiratorially.

And people actually believe this story. No, it's true. Not hundreds, not thousands, not a band of crazies – though, granted, many of them are crazy – but millions, billions of people, from all corners of the globe (if a globe can be said to have corners), over the course of two millennia, people actually believe this story. A story that defies the rules of logic and common sense, a story that defies the very laws of mathematics: $5 + 2 - 5000 = 12$. What sane, logical, rational, right-thinking person in the year of our Lord 2003, could actually believe such hocus pocus. Because this story – and trust me, this book is filled with stories even more outlandish – but this particular story was written nearly eighty years after the incident in question. Not by an eyewitness, not by a contemporary of Christ, but by someone who was not there, by someone who had not even been born yet. This is, I think, a pretty good definition of what the critics mean when they say "the unreliable narrator." It's like me telling you a story about something that happened in 1923. You'd have to be insane to believe my every word. Because this story lived for eighty years not as ink on paper, not pressed between the pages of a book, this story lived for eighty years as part of what the historians call the oral tradition. Which is another way of saying: as a series of rumors and gossip and hearsay and fiction. And we all know how stories, passed by word of mouth, can change and transform and mutate beyond all recognition over the course of eighty minutes, much less eighty years. And remember that this miracle, this so-called miracle, happened late in Christ's ministry. So the five thousand – or, let's be honest, more likely the five hundred – who flocked to see the Miracle Maker, the King of Kings, they'd heard all the stories before, they knew that when Christ speaks of nourishment and of of of satiety, that he's not speaking about food, that he's speaking metaphorically. In other words, they knew the script. And more than that, they knew their role in the drama. They were audience, yes, but they were players, as well. Therefore, when the baskets of food, the bread, the fish, were passed their way, they recognized that as their cue, and they knew their line to follow: "No, thank you. I'm full." And they passed it on. So this becomes a self-fulfilling prophecy. Anyone can feed an audience of five hundred or five thousand or even five million on five loaves of bread and two small fishes if the audience agrees not to eat the food. It doesn't take the son of God to accomplish that; it only takes a charismatic leader . . .

A drink of water.

. . . and willing followers.

A glance at the audience.

Ah, but what of the leftovers, you say! Five loaves of bread, twelve baskets of leftovers, is not this a miracle? We all know how something whole, something compact, takes up less space than something deconstructed. If you tear a loaf of bread into tiny pieces, there's now air that fills the space between the pieces, and it's really quite simple to fill two baskets with the crumbs of a loaf of bread that, when whole, filled only one. So much for miracles. And yet. And yet! People believe. Normal, average, everyday people like you and me actually believe these stories. Why? Is it because the stories in here are so compelling and convincing that one is compelled and convinced to believe what's up there? No, it doesn't work that way; it works the other way around. You see, people believe. They believe in Jesus, they believe in Allah, they believe in God, therefore they believe in the word of God. Regardless of what the words actually say, because if you believe in the storyteller, you will believe in the story.

A beat.

I'll say that again, for anyone who wasn't paying attention: If you believe in the storyteller, you will believe in the story. It's a Platonic paradigm, rather than an Aristotelian one, for all of you Ivy League graduates. You either believe or you don't, it's as simple as that. You see, in this postmodern, relativistic, shades-of-gray world, there are blacks and whites, there are yesses and nos, there are facts and untruths. You either believe or you don't. You either believe that Jesus fed five thousand with five loaves of bread and two small fishes, and he fed them until they were full, and there were twelve baskets of leftovers, you either believe or you don't. You either believe that Jesus made a blind man see and Jesus made a a a a deaf man hear . . .

Dramatically, but subtly, morphing into a Bible-thumping revivalist preacher.

. . . and Jesus made a mute man speak and Jesus made a crippled man walk, you either believe or you don't! You either believe that Jesus cured leprosy and Jesus cured dropsy and Jesus cured arthritis, you either believe that Jesus healed the mutilated and the feverish and the ill and infirm and demon-possessed, you either believe or you don't! You either believe that Jesus stilled the storm and walked on water and filled the fishermen's nets to bursting, you either believe or you don't! You either believe that Jesus raised Lazarus from the dead – four days dead, "Lazarus, come forth," he said, and he that was dead came forth – you either believe or you don't! You either believe that Jesus transformed bread and wine into body and blood, you either believe or you don't! It's either the truth about Jesus, or it's a story about a character who happens to be named Jesus! You either believe or you don't! And let me warn all of you who don't believe, all of you nonbelievers and disbelievers and unbelievers, and I know you're out there—I could hear you singing off-key. All of you skeptics and scoffers and doubters, all of you atheists and agnostics, you mathematicians and logicians, all of you secular humanists: let me assure you that by the end of the evening, you will believe. You will be converted, your leftovers will exceed your original amount. The person who walks out this door at the end of the evening will be a different person than the one who walked in, that is a promise, because? Because? What is the alternative? That the person who walks out that door at the end of the evening will be the same person who walked in, the same person seated in front of me at this moment, and let me tell you one thing I know about the person seated in front of me at this—let me tell you one thing I know for a fact about the person seated in front of me at this moment: that you want to believe. Whether you know it or not, whether you admit it or not, whether you fess up or not, you want to believe. And how do I know you want to believe, how do I know for a fact that you want to believe? Because, if you didn't want to believe, what in God's name are you doing here tonight?

A beat.

But there is, I fear, a Judas among us, and as Jesus said, "Woe unto that man." The enemy is in our midst, and people are not always who they appear to be. Are any of you cops? I said, are any of you cops? Because if you are, you must reveal yourself. Otherwise, it's entrapment, and I have eleven witnesses. A clever little ontological gambit with which the law has provided us lawbreakers, no? No one's a cop? NYPD, FBI, CIA, ATF, INS, IRS? No? No one's from the IRS?

No one's from the IRS.

Thank God. I need a drink.

Quickly refills glass with water, drinks. Complete tone and voice change.

Let me just drop the pretense, and say that now that we've established that none of you are cops, no one's going to arrest me, no one's from the IRS, let me just say that, between the thirteen of us, personally I don't believe. It's not that I actively disbelieve. I just think the question, "Does God exist?" – which, I think, is the question – and the search for an answer are irrelevant. That we, as human beings, by definition, are incapable of answering that question, so any time spent leaping up towards the heavens, trying to grab hold of an answer – and forgive me, any of you who do believe, but it strikes me as an utter waste of time. So, I was just putting on an act. And apparently not a terribly convincing one.

His phone rings.

It'll go to voice mail.

Which, after a few rings, it does.

Actually, more accurately, I was putting on half an—or a quarter of an act. Because the preaching, of course, was a total act, but the singing, I have to say, the singing was only half an act. I went to a boys' summer camp in the Adirondacks for years and years, where we were forced to learn these Protestant hymns, and I must know a hundred, a hundred and fifty, by heart. "I Love to Tell the Story," that's one of my favorites. Actually, it's not one of my favorites, I don't even really like that one, but it works thematically, and it's within my five-note range, so. Um, "Rock of Ages," that's probably my—I sing my kids to sleep every night with "Rock of Ages"—not tonight, of course, my wife's gonna sing them to sleep tonight. "Abide with Me!" Do you know "Abide with Me"? If you've ever heard five hundred sweaty boys, on a hot, humid August night, sitting back to back on the floor of a gymnasium, singing at the top of their lungs, unselfconsciously, "Abide with Me," if that doesn't make you believe, nothing will. When I'm buried, I want—just in case any of you decide to show up at my funeral, and just in case there's any dispute about my wishes – I would like the lone bagpiper on the distant hill to play "Abide with Me." And the funny thing is, I don't believe a word of these hymns, not a word. Well, I mean, they're just words, of course I believe them, they're just words, but you know what I mean, it's a figure of speech. I don't believe a word of them, and yet, for some ineffable reason, they provide me with a profound sense of strength and tranquility and and sustenance. So I was putting on a quarter of an act. Which doesn't make me an actor. Because I'm not, I'm a playwright. I've done this show for ten months now, and after every single performance, except for the first two, which really sucked, but after every other one, inevitably, invariably, during dinner—and it's going to happen tonight, trust me, one of you will pull me aside and say some variation of the following: "My God, you are such a brilliant actor." Thank you. In advance, thank you, truly, from the bottom of my heart. But I'm just playing myself. Although, that said, I don't want anyone to get the wrong impression. This is not one of those autobiographical, confessional one-person shows. Is there anything worse? That is the lowest form of theater. Trust me, not a single detail tonight is either autobiographical or confessional. It's just make believe. In fact – I was just thinking about this yesterday – the last time I was onstage – not that this is a stage, but – was my Senior year in high school. Fall of 19 … 79. Agatha Christie's "Witness for the Prosecution." Does anybody know this play? For those of you who don't – and for those of you smart enough not to admit it – "Witness for the Prosecution" is this awful – it's not awful, it's mediocre – this mediocre courtroom whodunit whose success is entirely contingent upon the audience not realizing that the young woman they see in Act Three is, in fact, the old woman they saw in Act One. Of course, in a high-school production, where everyone on both sides of the lights knows each other, what you get is not a ... whatdya call it? ... a coup de théâtre, as Dame Agatha envisioned, where the curtain is thrown back at the end to reveal the great surprise. In a high-school production of "Witness for the Prosecution," what you get is, five minutes after the curtain goes up, an audience full of moms and dads and brothers and sisters and grandmas and grandpas going, "How come Sally's wearin' a gray wig?" Anyway ... why did I tell that story? I'm sorry, I lost my place, shit, where was I?

> *Riffles through the script. After several seconds, if an audience member hasn't thrown out a line.*

Oh! "I'm not actor." Proof positive, I'm not an actor. Um, let me just say, briefly, you may have to bear with me tonight. It's been a really rough week. My head is sort of spinning. My daughter has been sick for the last few days, and last night we had a bunch of people over – like, fifteen, twenty, people – and it was really nice, it was supposed to be just wine and cheese and crackers and olives and, but it went til, God, 1:45, 2 o'clock, and then we cleaned up and I couldn't get to sleep, and I'm just exhausted. And then on top of all that, on, um, Thursday, I received a letter – overnight, certified mail – from the IRS, from some functionary at the IRS by the name of, I swear to God, Arthur Miller. "It's a letter from Arthur Miller! Oh, no, not that Arthur Miller." Mr. Miller wrote to say that he had seen a listing for "The Last Supper" in, of all places, the Village Voice. I know they still publish the Voice, but I didn't realize people actually read it. Anyway, Mr. Miller said that he had inferred from this listing that I was operating a theater and/or restaurant at 410 16th Street in Brooklyn. He wanted to inform me that this block, and my property specifically, is not zoned for commercial use, and that if, in fact, I was operating a theater and/or restaurant on said premises, that I would be in violation of – let me see if I can remember them all – federal, state and city tax codes; zoning laws; the city cabaret act; health-department and liquor-board regulations; as well as the bylaws of the Dramatists Guild and Actors Equity, neither of which I'm a member, so I have no idea what that was about. Furthermore, if I persisted in operating a theater and/or restaurant, I would be subject to prosecution and, if convicted, would face a fine and imprisonment. Not and/or. And imprisonment. Holy shit! I'm just trying to put on a show – like Mickey Rooney and Judy Garland in the backyard – and the government is after me. And, believe me, I've seen "Short Eyes," I've seen "Midnight Express," I've even watched a few episodes of "Oz." I know what happens to guys like me when they go to jail. So my lawyer – I'm forty years old; for the first time in my life, I've had to retain a lawyer – my lawyer has insisted that at the very beginning, I state that this is not a play, you are not in a theater, I am not an actor. Though I will be preparing and serving you a meal tonight, this is not a restaurant, I am not a chef. What you are witnessing – and this is the reason for all the religious rigmarole – what you will be participating in tonight is a religious service in a house of worship performed by a man of the cloth. I am, in fact, an ordained minister. In the Universal Life Church, headquartered in Modesto, California. www.ulc.net. Nine dollars and ninety-five cents, if I remember correctly.

Plucking a certificate off the refrigerator and passing it around.

Here are my Credentials of Ministry, just in case anyone thinks I'm pulling a fast one. And let it be known that I have, with the powers vested in me as a Universal Philosopher of Absolute Reality – my official title within the Church – the theological, if not necessarily the legal, right to conduct various religious ceremonies, not least among which is Holy Communion. I can preside at funerals, at weddings, baptisms, renewals of vows, and what we in the ULC affectionately call affirmations of love. So if anyone, after the performance – I'm sorry, after the service – if anyone is feeling particularly ... affirmative, you want to get married, or divorced, whatever, I'd be more than willing. For a nominal fee, of course. Which reminds me, quickly, payment. Since this is not a theater, there are no tickets. Since this is not a restaurant, there is no bill of sale. Payment is voluntary. You'll find in your programs an envelope marked "Offering." When you leave tonight, there's a collection basket at the door, my daughter's Easter basket, just drop your envelope in there, cash or check. Now, the suggested offering, which includes dinner and ... this, is twenty-five to fifty dollars, per person. Some woman last week asked me, "Is it twenty-five dollars for the back pews and fifty for the front?" "No, no, no." Here's the reason why there's a range. If I said, "Suggested offering: fifty dollars," then the people who could only afford twenty-five wouldn't come. Even though payment is voluntary, they wouldn't come. And I don't want to shut anyone out. There are people who can't afford more than twenty-five dollars, and I want to give everyone a chance to see this. I mean, the theater's elitist enough as it is – not that this is a theater – but you know what I mean, theoretically speaking, the theater's elitist enough, and I don't want to shut anybody out. But if I said, "Suggested offering: twenty-five dollars," then the people who could actually afford fifty – like all of you – would only pay twenty-five. So if I say, "Twenty-five to fifty," the people who can afford fifty … will pay fifty, and the people who can only afford twenty-five, because of peer pressure, self-loathing, whatever, are more likely to pay thirty, or even thirty-five dollars. I'm just trying to maximize profits. F-i, not p-h-e. And, finally, I apologize for making you enter through the back door tonight. But my lawyer has established that the front door is the legal and official entrance to my house, the back door is the legal and official entrance to my house of worship. Coincidentally, his law firm also represents Al Sharpton, and apparently the Reverend Sharpton has the same setup – a front door/back door thing, Al's house, Rev Al's Productions. And he's running for President, for chrissakes – is this a great country or what? – so I figure if Al Sharpton can get away with it, why not me? But see, in the end, I don't think this has anything to do with zoning laws and tax codes and health-department and liquor-board regulations. What I believe threatens them – Arthur Miller and his cronies – and my lawyer thinks I'm crazy, but what I think they find dangerous, what they ultimately accuse me of is blurring the line between theater and religion. Which presupposes, of course, that a line exists. But as I pointed out to Mr. Miller, in a letter I dashed off Thursday afternoon …

Taking the letter to the IRS off the refrigerator and reading it.

Let me read this, because I don't want to mess up any of these lines. "… that while religion is not typically theatrical, the theater is, at its very root, religious. Since the beginning of time, dramatic texts and performances have been intrinsically, inextricably linked to religious ceremony. The first ritualized performances of which we have record, in ancient Egypt …" – I know, it's pedantic as hell, but I was incensed – "… were religious ceremonies, in which deities were celebrated and glorified through sacrifice – originally human sacrifice, then animal, and finally metaphorical, representational sacrifice. The word 'tragedy,' of course …" – "of course," as if he'd know – "… derives from the Greek 'tragos,' meaning the goat sacrificed at the altar. The Greek theater, direct foreparent of our contemporary stage, has its origins in the celebration of a god – Dionysus, the god of birth and regeneration, of fertility and wine. The cult of Dionysus wore satyr costumes …" – or satyr, s-a-t-y-r – "… and chanted rhyming choric hymns, called dithyrambs, which later metamorphosed into the texts of the first so-called plays, and these costumed worshippers, half-human, half-goat, danced about an altar with such uninhibitedness that they were transported into an altered mental state called 'ecstasis.' The very nature of Greek tragedy, then, of all theater, Mr. Miller – and you should know this better than anyone …" – I have no idea if he'll get that joke – "… its moral and metaphysical concerns, its structure, its essence, is transformative and religious. The human impulse, the human need …"

Suddenly no longer looking at the letter, as if he's memorized this, or as if he really believes it.

"… better yet, the exclusively human need – to enact, to reenact, to characterize, to play, is inseparable from religion, from the act of religious veneration. Attendance at the theater has always been, is today, and forever will be public worship. This art form – the theater – is the art form of the gods, and we are supplicants at its altar. Sincerely yours, Ed Schmidt, Universal Philosopher of Absolute Reality."

Returns the letter to refrigerator, opens the script. Reads from the script.

"The Last Supper," a comedy, by … oh, and since this is not a theater, please, feel free to leave on any cellphones. And if you feel the need for a hard candy, now might be a good time to unwrap it, but fifteen, twenty minutes from now will be just as good a time. You're in church. Act accordingly.

Back to the script.

"The Last Supper," a comedy, by … and when I say comedy, I don't mean ha-ha, although laughs are good. Nor do I mean a Chekhovian comedy, where, ya know, someone pulls a gun and fires it and the bullet just misses, and somehow that's considered comic. When I say a comedy, I mean it in the strictest sense: a tragedy is any play in which the protagonist fails, a comedy is any play in which the protagonist succeeds.

Back to the script.

"The Last Supper," a comedy, by … I already did that part.

Turns the page.

There's one epigraph. Epigraph? Epigram. Epigraph. "The art of playwriting is the art of mixing oil and vinegar." Elmer Rice.

Turns the page. Describing the kitchen in which he stands.

"Act one. The setting is a kitchen. Along the back wall, custom-built, solid-birch cabinets and a stainless-steel countertop, a stove, dishwasher, sink, refrigerator, cellphone. A clock on the wall reads seven o'clock."

Looks up at the clock: 7:36.

Wow. 7:36. I didn't realize it's, um … awright, how bout this? "A clock on the wall reads seven-thirty-six. But it runs thirty-six minutes fast. Along one wall is a door and two windows, looking out on the backyard garden, where it is threatening rain. Along the opposite wall is a red velvet curtain, which separates the kitchen from the dining room and, beyond that, around the corner and to the right, a bathroom, whose toilet clogs easily and, for the successful completion of certain transactions, may require multiple flushings. Along the fourth wall is the … fourth wall. In the center of the kitchen is an island with a butcher-block countertop. At the island is a stool, on which sits an old woman, eighty-five years old, perhaps ninety, perhaps even older. She is disheveled, dressed in rags, and reeks of her own excrement." I had thought that (just parenthetically here) that, because I want the stench of this woman, or at least the thought of the stench of this woman, to so suffuse the room, I had considered, like fifteen minutes before you got here, that I would … there's really no delicate way of saying this … that I would take a shit on a plate, or in a bowl, and I would place it right here, where you couldn't see it, obviously, but you could smell it, and that way, when you entered, you'd just be swamped by this fecal tsunami. I know, it's disgusting, and needless to say, I've decided not to do that, I've decided instead to trust your conjurative abilities and your willingness to suspend disbelief in the moment, which, as Coleridge wrote, and I'm sure you're all familiar with the quotation, "which constitutes poetic faith" and imagine this …

Back to the script.

"… putrid old crone, seated on the stool, staring out the window, lost presumably in thought. In front of the old woman is a water glass, half-full …"

Refills the glass from the sink faucet, takes a quick sip before setting it down in front of the OLD WOMAN.

Or half-empty. "And her filthy, tattered hat."

He reaches into a drawer, pulls out a filthy hat, places it on the island.

"The curtain opens and the Mother enters. She is into her fifties, though don't ask how deeply. She wears an apron …"

He reaches into the drawer, pulls out an apron, puts it on.

Shit. I can't believe I forgot to, I meant to say this at the beginning. Because I'm going to play five characters, I've devised a sort of a costume shorthand. For the mother, I'll wear this apron. For the old woman, the filthy hat. For the daughter – she's, like, nineteen years old, nine months pregnant – I'll shove a pillow under my shirt. For the policewoman – a very small but crucial role at the end – I'll wear this …

Takes the child's fireman's helmet from the counter.

… actually, it's my son's fireman's helmet, but if I turn it around like this …

Does so.

… you can pretend it's a policewoman's hat. And for Judas – the one male character, who shuttles back and forth between the holy men in the dining room and the unholy women preparing the meal in the kitchen, I'm gonna wear a yellow jacket that – God, this is the thing I messed up last night. Judas wears a yellow jacket, but then at one point he gives it to the daughter, who exits with it, so, um … actually, ya know what, for Judas I'll do what I did last night, I'll use an accent. He'll start with the yellow jacket, but I'll do an accent, so when he gives the jacket to the daughter, you'll still be able to tell. OK. And one final … things change. And "The Last Supper" is a thing. Ergo, "The Last Supper" has changed. Not only from eight years ago when I first starting writing this, when it was supposed to be a real play with real actors on a real stage in front of a real audience – not that you're not real, but, you know what I mean, a real subscriber audience, average age ninety-four – but it's also changed since the summer, when I took time off to do rewrites, and it changes in small ways week to week. However, last week – there are three scenes, two character, dialogue scenes, that I'd been doing myself, playing both characters, and last week I finally concluded that they just don't work that way, that I can't do those scenes by myself, so for these scenes, um … I'm going to need a little help. But please, please, don't think of this as audience participation. I don't know about you, but I hate audience participation, if I hear there's audience participation, I won't even go. I dread it. "Tony 'n' Tina's Wedding," you couldn't pay me enough to go to that, so that's not what this is, it's not audience participation.

A beat.

What the hell, let's be honest, that is what it is, it's audience participation. But this is my kitchen! I'm your host, you're my guest. You have to trust me, everything I do tonight has a purpose. And believe me, anything any one of you is forced to do up here can't compare with what I'm doing voluntarily. I'm making an ass of myself, and I know it. And the fourth wall, there's no fourth wall, there never was a fourth wall, it's a phony concept, it doesn't exist.

Stepping past the island and back.

I'm here, now I'm here. Nothing broke! And besides, we don't all know each other, and we're all going to sit down to a meal afterwards, break bread together, we'll put on our masks, our social masks, ya know, we'll all be acting – that probably doesn't help – but I'm just going to need one man and one woman, let me just choose right now, so only those two have to spend the rest of the evening worrying.

To a woman.

Would you mind playing the female role? It's only two scenes, one has no dialogue, the other's six, seven lines, nothing difficult, exposition really.

She agrees.

Great.

To a man.

And would you mind doing the male role? One scene – like, four or five lines, but it's fairly crucial.

He agrees.

Good. Are you an actor?

He isn't.

Thank God. Because last night the guy was an actor, and it was disastrous. He was awful. It was so bad he nearly ruined the whole evening. Imagine that, this almost got ruined. And not to put any pressure on you, but I just want to make sure. That you don't suck. And I'm sure you don't, but I vowed, after this guy, that I wouldn't let it happen again. And don't think of this as an audition, please, but would you mind doing a quick scene? Just to make sure that you and I, that you're OK, that we're simpatico? Would you mind?

The man doesn't mind. Perusing his shelves as the man approaches.

Do you have any preference, comedy, drama … Shakespeare's probably out, right? Oh, I know! Right here.

Pulling a Samuel French edition off the shelf.

"Witness for the Prosecution." You play – actually, why don't you come over on this side …

The man stands behind the island, ED SCHMIDT *sits on the stool.*

I'm Robert Hearne, Detective Inspector, Criminal Investigations Department, New Scotland Yard, and you're Myers, Queens Council. It's a courtroom scene, we'll use them as sort of the jury. Right here. Skip this part, that's just the swearing in. From here. Oh, and can you do an English accent?

Ed Schmidt

The man hesitates.

No, forget it, there's no need. I shouldn't have asked. From here.

MYERS

Now, Inspector Hearne, on the evening of the fourteenth October last were you on duty when you received an emergency call?

HEARNE

Bad English accent.

Yes, sir.

MYERS

What did you do?

ED SCHMIDT

A beat, breaks character.

I'm sorry, ya know what, lemme just … it was fine, it was great, this is more for them than it is for you. You're Myers, right? Queen's council, which is prosecution. And I'm the eponymous witness for the prosecution. So we're on the same team. And we're both old pros. We've done this a thousand times, and on this specific, since it's such an important case, I've probably been up to your office three or four times to sip brandy and go over the testimony. So we've rehearsed this. I know the questions you're going to ask, you know the answers I'm going to give. We're acting off a script. But the trick is – and this is the magic of Agatha Christie, for those of you who don't know – we have to make it seem to them like this is a completely spontaneous exchange. So, in other words, you and I are playing roles – Myers and Hearne – but within the scene, Myers and Hearne are also playing roles. Not that you weren't doing it, but it's just something to keep in mind. For them more than you. OK? You can start from the top.

MYERS

Now, Inspector Hearne, on the evening of the fourteenth October last were you on duty when you received an emergency call?

HEARNE

Bad English accent.

Yes, sir.

MYERS

What did you do?

HEARNE

Even worse English accent.

With Sergeant Randell I proceeded to 23 Ashburn Grove. I was admitted to the house and established that the occupant, whom I later ascertained was Miss Emily French, was dead. She was lying on her face, and had received severe injuries to the back of her head. An attempt had been made to force one of the windows with some implement that might have been a chisel. The window had been broken near the catch. There was glass strewn about the floor, and I also later found fragments of glass on the ground outside the window.

MYERS

Is there any particular significance in finding glass both inside and outside the window?

HEARNE

The glass outside was not consistent with the window having been forced from outside.

ED SCHMIDT

Thank you, that was great.

The man returns to his seat, perhaps leads the audience in brief applause.

And it's fine that you didn't do the English accent, because Judas isn't English, so you won't have to, and I don't mean to brag, but you could probably tell, in high school my …

Spess-ee-ality!

… specialty was English accents. Before "Witness," I was …

Abysmal English accent.

… the Archbishop Thomas Becket in T.S. Eliot's "Murder in the Cathedral." In the great stone church on the grounds of the prep school …

Embarrassing English accent.

And before that, I was Freddy Eynsford-Hill, in "Pygmalion." Right! Howdedo!

End of accents, thank God.

Unfortunately, that's the last of the English accents you'll hear tonight. However, for the mother I will employ an Italian accent. But be forewarned, my Italian accent, and incidentally my French, somehow mysteriously, and rather quickly, morph into this quasi-Russian thing. I'll begin speaking like, I don't know, Jacques Cousteau, and by the end of the sentence you'd swear I was Solzhenitsyn. And what's strange is that the reason I gave up acting – or more accurately, the reason acting gave me up – was because I have this constitutional necessity to always be outside myself, always observing myself, I could never lose myself in the role, become the character, which is death for an actor, and one would think that an actor who's always watching himself act can also hear himself act. Apparently, I can't. So, regardless of whatever strange accent tumbles from between my lips tonight while I'm playing the mother, just imagine that it's a pitch-perfect, first-generation, Northwest-Tuscan, Meryl-Streep-"Bridges-of-Madison-County" Italian accent. OK.

Back to the script.

This is the last stage direction. "The mother opens …" – the old woman's here – "The mother opens the oven door and the room fills with the aroma of baking bread. It is the smell of home, of love, of comfort, of safety."

As the MOTHER, *he opens the oven door and pulls out a covered roasting pot.*

By the way, do any of you know Sullivan Street Bakery? They make this incredible rosemary bread …

He takes the lid off the pan and shows the guests a great loaf of bread.

… which I've been using for the last month or so. I'd heard about Sullivan Street, so I went in and there was this guy who was answering everyone's questions, so I introduced myself, and he introduced himself as Jesus. I said, "Hay-soos?" He said, "No, Jesus." I said, "You have no idea how well this is going to work." So I explained what I was doing, and I said, "What I want is not only for the bread to be warm when I serve it, but also I want the room to smell of rosemary, and how might I best accomplish that?" And Jesus said – and I have no reason to doubt the word of Jesus – Jesus said, "Put it in a covered roasting pot" – which is totally counterintuitive to me – "and turn the heat on, and the room will smell of rosemary." And it works! I'm going to turn the heat on – later, not now – and the room will fill with the aroma of rosemary.

He returns the bread and the pot to the oven.

Oh, by the way, I should have asked this at the beginning. Are any of you vegetarians?

The vegetarians identify themselves.

Anyone not eat red meat, but you will eat fish?

The pescatarians identify themselves.

Because what we're having tonight is fish. I don't know why I asked about red meat. Anyway. Red snapper, roasted red snapper. I ran into Chinatown early this morning, got two beautiful fish, rushed home, threw em in the refrigerator, so they're really fresh. And we have a big salad, a rice dish, plenty of wine and beer, the bread, dessert is great, and there's a vegetarian stew for— does that sounds OK?

Of course it does – it sounds delicious. To one of the vegetarians.

Can I ask, and I don't mean to single you out, but why are you a vegetarian? Is it philosophical, religious, health reasons?

Ed Schmidt

Improv response.

Because I have to say, I'm on your side. I mean, I eat fish – and red meat – so I guess I'm not on your side. But actually I am on your side, philosophically, because, like you, food has meaning to me. I think about what I eat. Unlike the rest of these Neanderthals, who'll shove anything down their throats. Because I believe – and I know this is going to sound like preaching, but this is my church, fuck off, I'm gonna preach – I believe that if you want to eat something, you have to kill it first. If you want to eat a fish, you have to catch it, watch it die, scale it, gut it, clean it, cook it, then you can eat it. If you want to eat bacon or buffalo chicken wings, you should have, at least once in your life, slaughtered a pig or a … buffalo? Because, for one, the food will taste better, that I guarantee. Any fish you catch yourself will taste better than anything at the fish market. If you grow your own vegetables, or even herbs on the windowsill, those will always taste better than anything you can buy at the supermarket. Because taste is not only what happens on the tongue. There's a vast context within which taste exists, and this will tie you to that context, it will make you aware of the cost of putting food on your table. And there is a cost. You will realize that the first step in that process is death, that your life, your nourishment, is dependent upon and inseparable from the death of another animal. And if you've done it, it's no longer a metaphorical conceit, it's a fact. And we're better off knowing that fact. It's not unlike what happened with Christ at the Last Supper. It was a Passover meal, after all, and Christ was literally the sacrificial lamb. "He took bread, gave it, and said, 'This is my body.' Likewise, he took the cup, gave it and said, 'This is my blood.'" Jesus didn't say, "Hey, guys, doesn't this red wine remind you of my blood?" he didn't say, "Let's pretend this bread is my body," no, "This is my body, this is my blood." If you want to benefit fully from the nourishment I can provide you – and when I say "I," I'm Jesus Christ – you must participate in the slaughter and cannibalization of me. Not a ritualistic act, but the thing itself. Which is, of course, where the Protestants and the Catholics differ. The Protestants see the bread and wine as symbols – which is reasonable – whereas the Catholics – the ever-entertaining Catholics – believe in transubstantiation. I'm not sure if you're familiar with this concept, but transubstantiation is the belief that the sacramental bread and wine are literally transformed into Christ's body and blood. Now, in order to believe in transubstantiation, you have to either be insane – which some of them are – or you have to willingly suspend your disbelief. You have to look at this wafer of bread, this cup of wine and say that's not bread, that's not wine. You have to take a leap of faith, and what is faith, after all, if not the belief that something is what it so obviously is not ... which is also the definition of irony. Anyway, it's easy to be skeptical and cynical and rational, it's easy to disbelieve, but in order to believe, to let go, to be vulnerable, to relinquish control, that ...

Not so gracefully gliding into the MOTHER*'s Italian accent.*

... -a takes-a great-a courage.

MOTHER

To the OLD WOMAN.

Would you like-a more water?

She retrieves the water glass, goes to the sink, fills it, places it in front of the OLD WOMAN. *She opens a drawer, begins humming "Rock of Ages," and slowly counts out thirteen spoons. She takes the spoons and exits to the dining room. Seconds later,* ED SCHMIDT *returns as* JUDAS, *wearing a yellow jacket. He rushes in, grabs the phone, dials, speaks conspiratorially.*

JUDAS

Bad gangster accent.

It's me ... Not yet ... He'll be here, trust me ... I don't know, about an hour or so ... No, that information's gonna cost ya ... I don't care what we agreed, now I disagree ... No, you want to know where, you want the exact address, you're gonna have to sweeten the pot ... Triple it. Ninety ... Fuck you, then ... Find him yourself ... Fuck you ... You fat fuck.

He hangs up, notices the OLD WOMAN, *pulls a pistol from his pocket, points it at her.*

Who are you? I'm gonna walk outta this room, old lady, and when I come back, if you're not gone, I'm gonna put a bullet through your head. And you tell them I want a new identity, new papers, new everything, or else I will personally track you down and

Ed Schmidt

I will kill you. And take a bath, for Chrissake, that's the worse plainclothes disguise I've ever seen.

> *He exits to the living room.* ED SCHMIDT *races downstairs, through the basement, and up through the back door, a small pillow shoved under his shirt, carrying a case of wine, as the* DAUGHTER. *She places the wine on the island, smells and sees the* OLD WOMAN.

DAUGHTER

What are you doing here? Mother! I told you I don't ever want to see you again. Mother! If you don't leave right now, I'm calling the police. Mother!

> *As she exits to the dining room.*

Mother, what is she doing here?

> ED SCHMIDT *quickly reenters, sits on the stool, and assumes the role of the* OLD WOMAN.

ED SCHMIDT

I'm going to be the old woman, very quickly.

> *She glances towards the dining room. With great difficulty, she slides off the stool, shuffles towards the wine, grabs the case, takes an unsteady step towards the backdoor, then suddenly stops. Playing* ED SCHMIDT *again.*

I'm sorry, I just, last night everyone was confused by this character, we spent forty-five minutes during dinner, the old woman, who is she, what she's doing, what's her deal? It seems obvious to me, too obvious, but at the risk of reducing this character to a single word, let me just say, she represents death. And earth. Each of the characters is assigned one of the elements. The old woman's earth; the mother – "Would you like-a more …" – she's water; Judas, of course, is fire. And also, and I'm sure this is clear to everyone, but the entire structural scaffolding of the text is based on the myth of Narcissus.

> *Blank stares.*

No? Jesus, OK, forget that part, forget it. We'll spend forty-five minutes tonight talking about that. Forget Narcissus. Death and earth.

> *He assumes the role of the* OLD WOMAN. *She grabs the case of wine, glances again towards the dining room, shuffles to the door, shoulders it open, and disappears outside.* ED SCHMIDT *rushes down through the basement, up into the dining room, and, as the* MOTHER, *reenters the kitchen. Still humming "Rock of Ages," she notices that the door is open, that the* OLD WOMAN *is gone, and that her filthy hat has been left behind. She picks up the hat, goes to the door, looks out, closes the door, places the hat on the island. She opens a drawer and begins slowly counting out thirteen forks. She glances at the clock. Let's say it's 8:02.*

Holy shit, it's 8:02. I didn't realize, let me just, normally I would act this out, the way it's written, but we're already, I'll just read the stage directions for this next scene.

> *Shuffles through the script to find the right place. Reading from the script.*

"The mother removes from the cabinets and drawers everything she'll need to set a table for thirteen. Thirteen spoons, forks and knives. Thirteen water glasses, thirteen wine glasses. Thirteen napkins. Thirteen bowls and plates. She does this …" – this is the important part – "… she does this in an orderly, ritualistic, almost ceremonial manner." Ideally, the setting of the table would take, like, twenty minutes. But we don't have twenty minutes. Let me just say, very quickly, the inspiration for this scene is that old Andy Warhol movie, a thirty-minute closeup of a guy's face while he's getting fellated offscreen, or belowscreen. I mean, you don't have to watch for more than ten seconds to get it – I get it, he's getting a blowjo— you know what, that's probably not the best example. Um … waves, waves, sitting on the beach, watching the waves! If you sit on a beach, watching the waves come in, for ten seconds, it's meaningless, or it has one meaning – the waves are coming in – and then you stand up and leave. But if you're forced to watch the waves for twenty minutes, we, as audience members, are incapable of watching the waves for twenty minutes and going, "Single meaning, single meaning, single meaning." What we do is, the passage of time forces us to impose metaphorical meaning onto the waves. Ya know, five minutes go by, and you start to think about the cyclical nature of the universe, the moon, the tides; ten minutes go by, you think about death and rebirth and regeneration; fifteen minutes of watching the waves and you think about your own mortality; twenty minutes, and you think, "What have I done with my life, why am I such a failure, I might as well put a gun to my head and kill myself." You see, the waves haven't changed, but we've changed their meaning. And that's what this scene is supposed to do – not the suicide part, but twenty minutes, no dialogue, the mother setting the table – and I know that sounds boring … and it is, actually – but after twenty minutes, these mundane, meaningless activities, you would impose profound metaphoric meaning on them, but since we don't have twenty minutes, you're going to have to imagine what those metaphors might be. And one more thing about this scene. The daughter comes back in, sits on the same stool where the old woman sat – maybe that's meaningful? – and you realize that the protagonist is me, not the daughter, I'm the protagonist, and for the protagonist you have to feel sympathy. Not sympathy, what's the word, it's like sympathy …

Invariably, a guest calls out, "Empathy?"

Empathy! Right, empathy! Wait a minute, is it sympathy or empathy? I always confuse those two. Are you sure, empathy? Let me check.

He grabs a dictionary off the shelf, opens it, starts paging through it, glances at the clock, closes the dictionary.

There's no time, I'll trust you, it's empathy. So you feel empathy for me. OK, so the mother sets the table, the daughter's here, and the mother finishes, and she exits into the dining room. Leaving the daughter alone. This is where I'm going to need you.

Calling up the female guest, guiding her to the stool.

… would you mind? You sit here. Two scenes, the first one is quick, no dialogue. It's just the daughter and Judas – I'm Judas – and I enter, and, um, in this scene there's no dialogue. Like I said. There is, however, a kiss.

A beat.

There's a lot of tongue. It's the kind of a kiss that, if no one else were here, would end with you and me – not you and me, the characters we're playing – just furiously going at it on top of the island.

The phone rings.

But I want you to know that, like I said, as an actor, I'm able to, ya know, and nothing personal, but I can emotionally distance myself.

The phone continues to ring.

I mean, while we're passionately making out, and I'm fondling you – and you can fondle me, too, it's fair game – to them it'll look like we're really going at it, but I'll, ya know, the whole time I can be thinking about, I don't know, regrouting the bathroom tiles or …

The phone continues to ring, now nine or ten rings.

I'm sorry.

He answers the phone.

Hello … Yes … Actually, I'm sold out through March 1st, but I do have a waiting list … No, Fridays and Saturdays only … Seven o'clock … You know what, this is not a good time to talk … Because I … I really can't talk … Because I'm in the middle of a show … Yes, yes, I am … That's OK. Ya know what, why don't you call me back in about two hours, ten, ten-thirty … We can discuss that then, I really have to go, I really do … Goodbye.

Hangs up, looks at the clock.

8:07. Jesus. Ya know what, it's so late, we're gonna have to skip the kiss. Is that OK? I'm sorry. We'll go on to the next scene. Here are your lines.

Hands her a page from the script.

So what happens, they're making out, Judas and the daughter, and in the middle of the kiss, the mother walks in, and Judas, being Judas, slithers off into the dining room and the mother is incensed. She starts getting dinner ready and the whole time she's staring daggers at her daughter. And one can assume that the child in her belly is probably Judas's, which, one can also assume, is probably not a good thing, from the mother's perspective. And remember, you had left the case of wine here, and the mother says …

                    MOTHER

Where is-a the wine?

                    DAUGHTER

Right there.

                    MOTHER

Where?

                    DAUGHTER

Right there.

                    MOTHER

I don't-a see.

                    DAUGHTER

I put it right there.

                    MOTHER

    Starting to sound Russian.

It is not-a right-a there.

                    DAUGHTER

Maybe you put it in the refrigerator.

                    MOTHER

    Solzhenitsyn.

I did not put anywhere. I have not seen the wine.

    Breaking character.

I'm sounding Russian, aren't I!?

Back to the MOTHER. *She pokes her head in the refrigerator. Italian accent again.*

Maybe your man-a steal it. He is drunkard and a thief. No good-a man. I do not-a trust him.

She looks but cannot find the wine. Long pause. When the head pokes out again, it belongs to ED SCHMIDT.

ED SCHMIDT

I'm sorry, I can't seem to find the ... is it my line?

Looks at the script.

"It is not here."

Back to refrigerator.

I can't ... I don't know ... I can't find the fish.

He stands back, looks anew at the open refrigerator. Forages again. Still no fish. After several desperate seconds, a thought dawns on him. He opens the freezer door. His head drops. He reaches into the freezer and pulls out two frozen fish, drops them on the island with a bang.

Fuck. Obviously, I meant to put them in the refrigerator.

He tosses the fish back in the freezer, tries to regroup. Finally.

Ya know what? Let's just take a break, five minutes, ten minutes, why don't we go into the living room, let me get my head together, I'll come up with something ...

And he moves the guests—and an assortment of beer, white wine, plastic cups, napkins, olives, half-consumed cheeses and pre-opened boxes of crackers, which, of course, are leftovers from last night's party—into the living room for intermission.

Ed Schmidt

INTERMISSION

After the audience is moved into the living room, ED SCHMIDT *turns the oven to 400°, takes the roasting pot (with bread) down to the basement, secretly replaces the bread with lamb stew that has come up to room temperature, returns to the kitchen, and puts the stew-filled pot into the oven. He places a few sprigs of rosemary, wrapped in cheesecloth, on the lid of the pot. He sets the vegetarian stew on the stove and begins reheating it.*

He returns to the living room and mutters something about "I have an idea, I think I can figure this out," then exits.

Meanwhile, downstairs, two assistants slice the bread and place it in two bread baskets, and they construct the salad on plates.

After about ten minutes has passed, ED SCHMIDT *returns to the living room, makes sure everything's OK – more wine, beer? – then hurriedly returns to the kitchen. It's possible that some of the guests will comment on how nice the rosemary bread smells.*

A few more minutes go by and he returns to the living room and gives some form of the following speech.

ED SCHMIDT

Good news and bad news. The good news is the vegetarians are gonna eat fine tonight. The bad news is the fish is definitely frozen. I tried thawing it, but it's gonna take way too long. I thought that I could throw something together, a pasta dish or something, but I discovered that the only thing I have enough of to feed this many people is macaroni and cheese. But then my kids won't eat for three weeks. So let me suggest, um, if I may, there's plenty of wine and beer, a big salad, the bread, rice, dessert, but I think the only way, if we're going to actually have a full meal, the only thing to do, I think, is to, um, to order out.

> *Reactions will range from dead silence to nervous laughter.*

There are a few options, but the best, and the easiest, is to, um, is pizza.

> *Reactions will range from even deader silence to even more nervous laughter. Once everything is worked out – how many pizzas, etc. – some version of this speech follows.*

And I know this goes without saying, but I'm gonna say it anyway. I know that when people come to something like this, that you come with certain expectations, especially about how much you're going to pay. I realize, tonight, all bets are off. So I will understand if, after you leave, if the envelopes are, ya know, slightly thinner than I'm usually used to. If you decide to give only forty-eight or forty-nine dollars each, I'll understand. No, truly, you expected a home-cooked meal and obviously you're not going to get that tonight. So, I'm not going to say another word, you know what I mean, about the payment. I'll order the pizza and see if they can rush it as quickly as possible.

> *He returns to the kitchen and pretends to call the pizza parlor. He returns to the living room and says something like the following.*

She said it'll be twenty, twenty-five minutes. Is it OK if, um – of course it's OK, it's my house – why don't we gather whatever you're drinking, whatever you're eating, we'll come back into the kitchen, and I'll do the last, like, twenty minutes of the show. If the pizza arrives late, if it arrives early, whatever, we'll deal with the timing.

> *Everyone gathers their things and returns to the kitchen.* ED SCHMIDT *reaches into the oven and surreptitiously removes the rosemary sprigs. He closes the red curtain separating the kitchen and the dining room. During Act Two, the assistants quietly set the table, light the candles in the chandelier, open the wine and water bottles, etc.*

Ed Schmidt

ACT TWO

ED SCHMIDT

I was just thinking, when you were out there and I was in here, running around with my head cut off, I was, um, does anybody remember those old Scholastic Books, the order forms? I loved those, I always ordered the sports books, baseball books, especially. I remember, my favorite book was "Miraculous Ninth Inning Comebacks!" "They were eleven runs behind …" but then when I was, I had to be eight, because we were in Wisconsin then, I went through this very brief obsession with cooking, or baking, actually. Cookie-baking. I baked those— you remember those peanut butter cookies? Where you pressed down with a fork, then turned it ninety degrees to make a grid? I must have made tens of thousands of those. And you know how certain foods have meaning, to this day, whenever I see those peanut butter cookies, I'm literally a child again. Anyway, I fairly quickly tired of cookies, and I realized I wanted to make a real adult meal for real adults. So my mother, God bless her, got together three other couples. Dinner for eight. Actually, it was lunch, I was eight years old, I couldn't stay up late enough to make dinner. Sunday lunch, we went to Saturday night Mass. And I decided to make my favorite dish – Chinese Pie. Which was essentially shepherd's pie. Mashed potatoes, ground beef, corn or peas. Not until I was twenty-one did I realize, Chinese people don't eat this food. It was my mother's idea of fusion cooking, in 1970. And my mother had two approaches to cooking – cold casseroles and hot casseroles. And all of her recipes were on little index cards. And each casserole was layered, and they had a unifying layer. For the cold casseroles, the unifying layer was usually mayonnaise. A layer of mayonnaise, layer of chopped iceberg lettuce, another layer of mayonnaise, grated carrots, mayonnaise – it was called seven-layer salad, I just remembered that. Seven-layer salad, four of which were mayonnaise. In Chinese

Pie, the unifying element was mashed potatoes. A layer of mashed potatoes; a layer of what my mother called hamburg – which was ground beef sautéed well beyond well done; another layer of mashed potatoes; a layer of corn – frozen, of course, and boiled not only til all the flavor but all the nutrients had leeched right out of it; mashed potatoes; and then the coup de grâce – crumbled potato chips and grated Kraft cheese. So you get a crunchy top! Oh, I loved it. So I spent all Sunday morning making Chinese Pie, and I can remember taking the casserole into the dining room, and then I can't remember – and, obviously, I remembered this story because it's a food-disaster story – so, I can't recall whether I stayed in the dining room or I was too anxious and I ran back into the kitchen, because the next memory I have is of being in the kitchen, with my mother, and I'm tasting the Chinese Pie, and I know something has gone drastically wrong. It was foul. And my mother – infinitely patient – she said, "Well, let's look at the index card and see what you did wrong." And I said, "It wasn't me, Mom! I followed the recipe exactly—" I haven't changed in thirty-two years – "It can't be my fault, it's gotta be somebody else's …" She said, "Did you do the hamburg?" "Yes." "Did you do the corn?" "Yes." "Did you do the potatoes?" "Yes, Mom, just like it says: two pounds of potatoes, cold water, bring it to a boil, mash them, stick of butter, half teaspoon of pepper, cup of salt …" It said a teaspoon of salt. I put in a cup. And it was that old Morton's salt – you remember, with the aluminum flip-top? A cup of salt, I was mortified. And my mother – my mother's a wonderful person, though I've never considered her to be particularly wise, but on this day, she had words of wisdom. She said, "It's only a meal. You have three meals a day, a thousand a year, you have eighty thousand meals over the course of your life. If this one's no good, there are seventy-nine thousand, nine hundred and ninety-nine more." Yeah, but why does mine have to be the one that's inedible? And then she said, and these are the words I'll never forget, she said, "The least important part of a meal is the food." Twenty-one years of Chinese Pie, I can attest, to my mother, the least important part of a meal was the food. But then she said, "What's more important is who you're sitting next to, what you talk about, what the lighting's like, what happened before the meal, what's going to happen after the meal. The least important part of a meal is the food." And when I was in here, trying to thaw the fish, I thought, Jesus Christ, we're gonna put that theory to the test tonight. And I tried to remember, how did it end? Was there a happy ending? Did my mother save the day somehow? I have no idea, I can't remember, but I thought, maybe I should tell you we ordered pizza and everybody lived happily ever after. But I don't think, in Beaver Dam, Wisconsin, in 1970, that pizza delivery had been invented yet. Anyway, lemme quickly synopsize where we were. The mother has just discovered that the wine is missing. She also discovers that the fish is frozen, but that's another story. So at first, she blames the daughter for never having gone to the wine store.

Without doing any accents.

"Of course I went to the wine store, mother. Look, here's the money you gave me …"

Taking his wallet out.

"… you can count it, there's a hundred dollars less." "Well, then your man must have stolen it." "My man didn't … Judas, come in here! Did you steal my mother's wine?" "Steal your mother's, of course I didn't steal your mother's wine." "Well, all I know is there's no wine, and you can't have a meal without wine, so one of you is going to have to go back to the wine store and get more wine." And Judas says, "I have an idea. Give me one minute with your daughter." Now, the mother's seen what can happen when Judas and her daughter are left alone for less than one minute, but, against her better judgment, she goes into the dining room, leaving them alone. And Judas says to the daughter …

To the man who was supposed to play JUDAS.

This was your big scene. I'm sorry, but we're gonna have to skip over it.

Back to the play.

So Judas says, "Look, this place is gonna be very dangerous in about a half hour." Meaning, of course, that the Romans, who he's been negotiating with on the phone, are coming to arrest Christ. He doesn't say any of that, but he says, "It's gonna be very dangerous. I don't want you here. I want you to leave. Take your mother's money. But don't go to the wine store – I'll tell her that you did – don't go to the wine store, go to the prearranged spot." Obviously, they have a plan. "Go to the prearranged spot. I'll take care of everything here, and then I'll meet up with you later." And it's started to rain, so he gives her his yellow jacket. So the daughter leaves with her mother's money and Judas's jacket. The mother returns. "Where is-a my daughter?" "She went to the wine store." Which is pleasantly surprising to the mother, it's not what she expected. So she starts preparing the fish, which, obviously, I'm not going to do tonight. Five minutes go by, ten minutes go by, no sign of the daughter. Presumably, the wine store is just around the corner. Fifteen minutes go by, still no sign of the daughter, she looks out the window, opens the door, looks out, she's starting to get worried. Twenty minutes go by, the fish is ready to go in the oven, still no sign of the daughter. She picks up the phone, calls the wine store. "Was my daughter there?" "Oh, yes, she was here about three hours ago." "No, was she there in the last twenty minutes?" "No." She hangs up, now she's suspicious, she knows something's up, and she knows Judas is behind it. And just as she's about to confront Judas, the doorbell rings. It's Jesus and the guys. So the mother exits, to open the door for Jesus and his disciples. Leaving Judas alone.

JUDAS

Picks up the phone, dials. Gangster accent.

It's me ... Yeah, they're here ... Lemme check. Yeah, he's here ... Thirteen, including me. And there's a lady, but don't worry, I'll take care of her ... I told you, you want that information, you want the exact address, you're gonna have to ... Bullshit ... You're bluffin, you have no idea where I am ...

Nervously looking out the window.

Is that a threat, are you threatening me? Ya know what, deal's off. Deal's off.

JUDAS slams the phone down. Pause. Regains his composure, exits into the dining room.

Hey, Jesus, how ya doin!

After a few seconds, the MOTHER *enters, wearing the apron, starts puttering around the kitchen, then stops.*

ED SCHMIDT

Let me just, because I don't want to disappoint anyone, or add to your already profound sense of disappointment, but this play – and, ya know what, screw Arthur

Ed Schmidt

Miller, it's a play, arrest me, it's a play – this play does not have a happy ending. Which, now that I say it, is pretty much exactly what we could use right now. Because I think it's impossible, by definition, to write a great play that ends happily, because the one central, indisputable fact about life is that it ends unhappily. And any work of art that denies or, even worse, ignores that fact is dishonest and immoral. And call me pretentious, but when I sit down to write a play, I attempt to write a great play. Occasionally, I fail. Because it's the duty of art, or one of the many duties of art, to remind us of this fact, that we don't live happily ever after. Because everything we do in our daily routines, the fact that we have daily routines, that we wake up, we go about our daily routines, we go to sleep, we wake up the next morning, we go through our routines again, everything about that implies that we do believe in happy endings, we do believe everything works out in the end. What we do is we delude ourselves, we willingly suspend our disbelief, and not just in the moment, but in a million consecutive moments, we trick ourselves into thinking that what we do, what we spend our days doing, matters, that somehow we're going to change the world. But, ya know, unless we're Shakespeare, which we're not, unless we're Leonardo or Escoffier, which we're not, we're not going to change the world. The chances of what we do, of the product of our labor, outliving our own selves, or even outliving the vague memories of vague relatives, is nil. Nil! And yet, if we admitted that … I mean, when I sit down to write a play … well, I can't convince myself it's going to be Shakespeare, Shakespeare's up here, Shakespeare's God – I guess, I do believe in God. But if I'm honest with myself, which I rarely am, I know it's not going to be Chekhov or Beckett or Wilder or O'Neill or Miller – not the IRS, the real Arthur Miller – the best I can reasonably hope for when I sit down to write a play is Elmer Rice. I joke with my brother, he writes novels, I say, "Your life changed when you realized you'd never be Kafka, whereas my life changed when I realized I'd never be Elmer Rice." You have no idea who Elmer Rice is. Nor should you. Elmer Rice was a very famous playwright in the '20s and the '30s and '40s – wealthy, famous, critically acclaimed – and now he's utterly forgotten. Flushed down the pipes, thrown out with the ashes and potato peels, buried underneath the rubble, one more for the scrapheap. Which is the point, after all. I mean, some mornings I wake up – actually, every morning I wake up, but some mornings after I wake up – I take my kids to school, I come home, I go upstairs to my office, and I start writing, writing my plays, out loud, talking to myself, doing the lines out— in funny voices, I talk to myself in funny voices. This is what I do. I hesitate to say this is what I do for a living, but this is what I do, I talk to myself in funny voices. And on those rare days when I take a step back, a half, a quarter-step back, I see this man, forty years old, in his windowless office, his wife is at work making an honest living (with health benefits, thank the Christ), his kids are joyfully playing at school, the sun is shining, the birds are chirping, and here he is sitting alone, talking to himself in funny voices. For six hours a day. And I think, how ridiculous is this? And what's even more ridiculous is that this man – me – thinks that what he's doing – talking to himself in funny voices – is somehow a useful and meaningful way to spend a day, much less an entire life. Which is beyond ridiculous, it's pathol— it's crazy. Let's be honest, it's crazy. And then I take my lunch break, I come downstairs, make myself a sandwich, glass of water, and I open the newspaper – I give myself a half hour to read the newspaper – and I read about [two or three stories currently in the news, i.e.] the inevitable war, I think, in Iraq; about the insanity between the Israelis and the Palestinians, and if I allowed myself to place what I'm doing in my little office in the greater context of the world I'm reading about, I wouldn't be able to climb back upstairs and continue talking to myself in funny voices. The only way I can do that is to convince myself that what's going on up there matters, if I allowed myself five minutes to look out the window, to truly see, the wonders and the joys and the miracles of life – and I'm not being sentimental here, it cannot be denied, that this Earth and our place on it are wondrous, awesome things – and this is how we choose to spend our time on Earth. This is how I've chosen to spend my time on Earth: Talking to myself in funny voices. And consider for a moment how you have chosen to spend your time on Earth, consider how you've chosen to spend this very evening – listening to me talk to myself in funny voices. And you're going to pay me for the privilege. Which is more ridiculous than what I do. Because if you had any guts, any guts at all, if you valued your life a pennysworth, if you truly understood how precious and fragile and fleeting life is, I swear to God, you would stand up right now and you would say, "What in God's name am I doing here listening to this raving mediocrity?" and you would leave! You would stand up and leave! But don't, it's in the script, it's part of the script. You would do something! Because character is action, yes? That's Aristotle. You are what you do. Character is action. What is your action? Sitting here, listening to me talk to myself in funny voices, waiting for a fucking pizza, that is your action, what does that say about your character? Don't answer, because I know. I'll tell you what it says about your character. It says that you do believe, you do have faith, it'll all work out in the end, it has meaning, we'll all live happily ever after, and who can blame you? Because what is at the root of all belief, all faith, all systems of religion, if not, "They lived happily ever after." Life on earth may be difficult and painful and joyless, but in the end, up there, in the ever after, there'll be milk and honey, a chicken in every pot, there'll be forty virgins for every martyr. But you know as well as I do, that there are no miraculous ninth-inning comebacks, you know as well as I do that there are no magical multiplications of food, that, in the end, oil and vinegar do not mix, that there will be no deus ex machina, descending from the heavens to save the day, no coup de théâtre, where the curtain is thrown back to reveal the great surprise, you know as well as I do that there is no cure for a cup of salt!

>*A beat.*

And yet! And yet. I have come to the conclusion – and I'm sure this is just a rationalization, so please, don't disabuse me of this fantasy, it's pretty much all I have left – I have come to the conclusion that this . . .

>*"Witness for the Prosecution."*

. . . or this . . .

>*"The Last Supper."*

. . . or better yet, this …

>*The dictionary.*

This is proof, more than any so-called holy text, proof of our need to believe. And when I say need, I don't mean psychological shortcoming – "He's so needy" – I mean necessity, the necessity to believe, of literally it goes without saying. We live in this world, we experience it, we sense certain things, call them what you will – joy or terror or love or yellow – and we human beings, we resilient and resourceful human beings, we create an elaborate system of signs and symbols called language, not so much to communicate these vague things to others, but above all to communicate them to ourselves. We assign them words, we reduce them to words, we name the unnamable, define the indefinable, we eff the ineffable, we try to capture these elusive, fluttering

... what's the metaphor? Leaves, falling leaves, no butterflies, yes, butterflies, because they're just out of reach and we need a tool, so that we can net them and mount them and pin them and label them with indelible ink, so that we can step back and say, "Ah, yes, this is love. This is terror. This is yellow." We translate these things from one language – the infinitely complex language of sensation and experience and being – into the finite language of the American Heritage Dictionary. And the more complex and subtle we make the system – through metaphor, through irony, through style – above all, through style – the more books we publish, the thicker the books become, and the more we realize how gaping is the chasm between the words in here and the not-words out there, between that which we define and that which we know. And it is in that gap, in that unbridgeable abyss, between the yes and the *I don't know*, that is where God exists. Not here, and not here, but somewhere in the middle, right about where Elmer Rice lives. And every time we attempt to span that gap, to leap from here to there, every time we act, every time we play, every time we ... we ... we search for the right word, every time the fog clears and the mist shifts and the cliffs comes into view, high and seductive and perilous, suddenly, briefly, the cliffs come into view, and we take a step back and we take a deep breath, and we start forward, one foot in front of the other, gaining speed, the wind against our face, and we plant our foot at the edge of the cliff, our cliff, and we leap. And we leap! And we fail and we fall and we're caught. That is when we, a thousand times a day, whether we know it or not, whether we admit it or not, whether we fess up or not, that is when we, in that futile leap, that we reveal, that we confess that we believe.

> *He simulates a knock on the backdoor by rapping on the island. The* MOTHER *opens the door.*

MOTHER

May I-a help you?

POLICEWOMAN

> *Donning the fireman's helmet; he carries* JUDAS's *jacket and the* MOTHER's *wallet.*

Good evening, ma'am. Do you know who this belongs to?

Hands her a wallet.

MOTHER

This is-a mine.

POLICEWOMAN

And the picture of the young woman inside?

She opens the wallet, looks at the photograph.

MOTHER

This is-a my daught— what has … has something happened to my daughter?

POLICEWOMAN

Your daughter was mistaken. By the police. She was wearing this jacket. She was mistaken for someone we've been looking for, a very bad man. Your daughter was shot. She is dead.

Quick removes the fireman's helmet, rushes into the dining room, immediately returns as JUDAS.

JUDAS

Seeing the POLICEWOMAN.

What the hell are you …?

He pulls his pistol, points it at the POLICEWOMAN.

How did you know where I was?

Moving past the MOTHER.

Excuse me. Tell me! How? Wait a minute, is it just you? Are you the only one? Where are all the other— there are thirteen of em! What the hell is goin on here? What the hell …

Quickly becomes the POLICEWOMAN, *shrugs, raises her hands, palms up; she has no idea what he's talking about.*

ED SCHMIDT

Bang! The front door is battered wide open. It flies off its hinges. We can hear the sound of a dozen policemen storming the house to arrest Christ and the—

The doorbell rings.

We can hear the sound of the pizza guy.

He dashes through the dining room towards the front door.

Can you get that? It's the pizza! Do you have money?

His wife, presumably, clomps downstairs and pretends to pay the pizza guy. He dashes back into the kitchen, resumes.

We can hear the sound of a dozen policemen storming the house to arrest Christ. The policewoman pulls her pistol and rushes into the dining room. Judas turns, starts towards the door, stops, sees the jacket, his jacket, blood-covered, realizes what has happened, realizes what he has done, realizes that there is no escape. He turns, sits on the stool, pulls his gun, drops it in front of him, drops his head. The mother, stunned, moves towards the commotion.

He exits into the dining room, rushes downstairs, through the basement, through the back door and into the kitchen, and assumes the role of the OLD WOMAN, *a half-empty wine bottle in one hand. She takes a glug, looks around, spots her hat on the island, shoves it on her head, turns to go. She notices* JUDAS, *sitting in the stool, head bowed. With great sentiment, she shuffles over to him, places the half-empty wine bottle on the island in front of him, and turns to go. Before she reaches the door, she smells the bread. She glances back towards the dining room, quietly opens the oven door, takes out the roasting pot – which the audience assumes is filled with the loaf of bread – closes the oven door, exits through the back door.* ED SCHMIDT *rushes through the basement, upstairs, into the dining room – where he hands the pot of reheated stew to the assistants, who quietly ladle the stew into the bowls – and enters the kitchen as the* MOTHER. *She walks to the counter, picks up the wallet, opens it, looks at the photograph of her daughter.*

MOTHER

Singing "Abide with Me."

"Abide with me, fast falls the eventide,

The darkness deepens, Lord with me abide.

When other helpers fail and comforts flee,

Help of the helpless, O abide with me."

> JUDAS *lifts his head to hear the hymn. He sees the wine bottle in front of him. Where did that come from? He considers it, lifts it to his lips, drinks, sets it back on the island with a thump. The* MOTHER *turns at the sound of the thump, sees the wine bottle, grabs it,* to JUDAS.

It was-a you. You steal-a the wine.

> *(She spies the pistol, picks it up, points it at* JUDAS. *She can't pull the trigger. She looks at the photo of her daughter, staggers to the backdoor, stops, bows her head, long pause. She turns, the gun pointed at* JUDAS, *and pulls the trigger. BANG!)*

ED SCHMIDT

The man's body falls in a pool of his own blood. And the room fills with Romans.

> *As he turns off the flame under the simmer vegetarian stew and takes a small, hidden loaf of bread from the counter and places it at the front of the island.*

And the woman turned to the sinners, took bread, gave it and said, "This is not my body."

> *As he moves the half-empty wine bottle next to the bread.*

Likewise, she took the cup, gave it, and said, "This is not my blood. What you see before you is a meal, one among tens of thousands. It is not a metaphor, it is not a story, it is not a testament of anything. It is the thing itself – a flawed meal prepared by an imperfect mortal. It will pass through you, this bread and wine, be transformed into waste, and then be gone. It may fill your belly, but it will not nourish your soul. It will not cleanse your sins or heal the wound or ease the pain or stem the flow of blood. This meal will not save you, it will not satisfy your longings, it will not grant you everlasting life. And yet. Without it, you will surely perish." Come. Let us eat and drink. You either believe or you don't.

> *The curtain miraculously opens to reveal a dining table set with a lit-candle chandelier, bottles of wine and water, salad on plates, bread in baskets, and lamb stew in bowls, and* ED SCHMIDT *disappears out the back door.*

THE END

sort of ...

Ed Schmidt

DINNER

Conspicuously propped near one of settings is a prayer sheet that reads …

Please read this aloud after everyone is seated.

Make yourselves at home.

The empty bowls are for the vegetarians and for any carnivores who don't eat lamb.

There is more lamb stew in the pot and more beer in the refrigerator.

If you prefer a more Biblical mood, you can turn off the kitchen lights.

I will return in about fifteen minutes to join you and give coyly evasive answers to all of your questions.

If you would like to say grace, might I suggest the following:

*Let us raise our heads in prayer. To the
willing suspension of disbelief in the
moment, which, as Coleridge wrote, and I'm
sure we're all familiar with the quotation,
constitutes poetic faith. Amen.*

MY LAST PLAY

Cast & Productions

My Last Play opened on November 13, 2010, in Ed Schmidt's basement apartment, at 29 4th Place, Brooklyn, New York. It closed on June 19, 2011.

The play was later performed five times in 2011, from September 28 to October 3, at the PowerHouse Arena, 37 Main Street, Brooklyn, New York.

In both productions, Ed Schmidt played the role of ED SCHMIDT.

MY LAST PLAY

ED SCHMIDT's book-lined living room. Ten to fifteen chairs. Bookshelves with nearly two thousand theater books. A staircase up to the rest of the apartment. Ten to fifteen chairs, arranged in rows.

While the audience enters and sits, ED SCHMIDT *comes and goes. He greets everyone, informs them of the location of the bathroom. He might vacuum a bit, or arrange chairs, or straighten books in the shelves. After everyone has arrived and taken seats, he exits into another room. A minute or so later, he enters, agitated.*

ED SCHMIDT

Par la mort non de diable, si j'étais que des médecins je me vengerais de son impertinence …

He coughs two or three times.

… et quand il sera malade, je le laisserais mourir sans secours. Il aurait beau faire et …

Cough, cough.

… beau dire …

Cough, cough, cough.

… je ne lui ordonnerais pas la moindre petite saignée, le moindre petit lavement; et je lui dirais …

Cough, cough, cough, cough. He pulls out a handkerchief, coughs lustily, coughs up blood into the handkerchief.

"Crève! …"

He coughs, falls to floor.

Ed Schmidt

"... Crève!"

He dies. Long pause. He jumps to his feet.

This isn't real! I'm not dead! I was only acting!

Bows.

Thank you, thank you. Those were the last words spoken by Jean Baptiste Poquelin, better known as Molière. The year was 1673 and Molière was dying of tuberculosis, and he knew it, so he wrote himself a play that could accommodate a lead actor prone to sudden, violent, tubercular coughing fits. The name of the play was "Le Malade Imaginaire." "The Imaginary Invalid." And his role was Argan, the hypochondriac extraordinaire. Late in the third act of the fourth public performance of "Le Malade Imaginaire," Molière coughed up blood into a handkerchief, lost consciousness, hit the floor, was dragged through the curtains, backstage, and died.

Shows the audience the bloody handkerchief.

This is Molière's actual handkerchief. No, it is! I bought this in Paris in 198— no, 96, outside the Comédie Française, a little side street, a tiny French bookseller, who, when he discovered that not only was I a Molière aficionado, but, even more importantly, an American, he reached underneath the table and he pulled out this handkerchief and he told me the story of the death of Molière. "C'est vrai," he said. "C'est la vraie chose." "It's real. This is the real thing." And for twenty-five francs, who was I to doubt him?

Recreating the scene.

In the scene that you just saw me so convincingly reenact, Argan is arguing with his brother Béralde, and Béralde has just said, "Brother, you are not sick. You are, in fact, a hypochondriac, and your doctors are an army of quacks. And in order to help you see the light, I am going to take you tonight to the theater, to see a play, a comedy, on this very subject, the unscrupulousness of the medical profession, and this play happens to be written by a fellow named Molière. So, Argan responds angrily, because Molière was famous for having publicly humiliated doctors, patients and the entire medical profession for decades from the stage, so Argan says, "Par la mort non de …" "By the death of …"— it's an idiomatic expression, I translate it as "As the devil is my witness." "As the devil is my witness, if I were of the medical profession, I would pay him back" – meaning Molière – "I would pay him back for his impertinence. And when he was sick, I would let him die without lifting a finger. He could say or do anything he liked, I would not prescribe for him the tiniest bleeding or the briefest enema. I would say to Molière, 'Crève! Crève!'" "Choke, die!"

Pause.

So, the real Molière, playing the fictional Argan, is telling the fictional Molière to "Die, die!" at which point the real Molière takes his advice and actually goes ahead and dies. Now, since Molière was playing a hypochondriac, the audience assumed this was part of the show, that he was acting, and since "Le Malade Imaginaire" is a comedy, the audience laughed as Molière died. I'd like to think that Molière – if he hadn't actually been dying at the moment – would have appreciated the irony. So he was dragged back through the curtain. A minute later, out came a woman, in full costume, a member of the company – this was Molière's wife – she said, "The great Molière has fallen ill! Is there a doctor in the house?" Which is, incidentally, where the phrase "Is there a doctor in the house?" comes from.

Pause.

At least that's what the bookseller told me. "Is there a doctor in the house?" Well, of course, there were several doctors in the house, all there to see the latest scandal, the latest satirical screed from that bastard Molière's pen, but the last thing any doctor wanted to do for an ailing Molière was to help him get better. So not a single man raised his hand. Madame Molière rushed backstage, reemerged another minute later, the handkerchief in her hand, dabbing at her tears. As the French bookseller told me …

Bad French accent.

"Sometimes ze stage blood and ze stage-a tears is-a real." That was more Italian than French, wasn't it? At any rate, she rushes out and says, "The great Molière is dying!

Is there a priest in the audience to hear his final confession?" There was, in fact, one priest, dressed in his priestly vestments. However, as the audience turned to the priest, Molière was also famous for having publicly humiliated priests and religion from the stage for decades, so the last thing any priest wanted to do for a dying Molière was to help him get into heaven. So the priest said the first thing that popped into his head, which was, "C'est un costume! C'est un costume!" "It's a costume! It's a costume!" The audience didn't believe him. He ran for the exit, they intercepted him. He resisted. He threw knees, feet, fists, elbows, one of which caught an elderly woman across the bridge of the nose, spilling blood everywhere. She fell to the ground, the audience parted, at which point no fewer than four men said some version of the following: "Step aside! I am a doctor!" Thereby revealing themselves not only as doctors but liars. The audience jumped on the doctors. The priest saw daylight, again rushed for the exit, again was intercepted, again resisted, was lifted over the heads of the audience, passed forward and dumped unceremoniously at the feet of Madame Molière. She lifted him up, rushed him backstage to hear Molière's final confession. The priest was two minutes late. Molière was dead. An unredeemed sinner, at the age of fifty-one.

Pause.

I'm forty-eight, in case anyone's keeping score. I am not dying of tuberculosis. I do, however, suffer from migraines. I have occasional dizzy spells. Lately, I've been having this worrisome sort of tightening in my chest. I've had it checked out – there's a history of heart disease in my family – my doctor has assured me there's nothing to worry about.

Pause.

At least for now. A few months ago, I had a small growth removed from my calf – it's non-cancerous. My eyesight is fading rapidly, my memory is developing wider and more numerous gaps, I eat too many processed foods, I don't exercise regularly, but, all in all, for a forty-eight-year-old man, I am in good physical condition. There is, in other words, no reason for me to write a play in which the lead actor might drop dead at any moment.

Pause.

Although one never knows. Karel Capek, the great Czech playwright, died at forty-eight of double pneumonia. Bulgakov was felled by the same kidney disease that took his father. He was forty-eight. Sidney Howard, one in a long, long list of mediocre, forgettable American playwrights, was crushed to death by a tractor on his farm at the age of forty-eight. So, this is my last play. I hope it is by choice and not by accident.

 Pause.

Now, when I call this my last play – I'm not, it's not really a play, I'm not sure what to call it, because a play first and foremost must be a work of fiction. Fictional characters, fictional setting, fictional dilemmas, fictional lives and deaths. The one goal I set myself when I first started to write this was that there would be no stories, that everything would be real, everything would be true. So, it's not a play. I'm not sure what to— let's, for argument's sake, let's just call it "My Last Play."

 Pause.

"My Last Play." I wrote my first play when I was sixteen. After a failed love affair. I've written twenty-nine plays, nine of which have received professional productions. And when I say professional, that doesn't necessarily mean that I was paid. Two of my plays have been published. Two. In thirty-two years. So that should give you some indication of what you're in for tonight.

 Insistent.

But I have given my life to this pursuit, this calling – playwriting – to the theater, and the theater has not given me enough in return, and so I am walking away from it.

 Pause.

Now, retiring from playwriting at the age of forty-eight is not unprecedented in the annals of the stage. Shakespeare wrote his last play, "The Tempest," at forty-eight, and then he, too, for all intents and purposes – to use a phrase that Shakespeare himself coined: "for all intents and purposes" – he walked away from the stage. Shakespeare died four years later, at the age of fifty-two.

Pause.

Did I mention I'm forty-eight? Shakespeare at fifty-two, Molière at fifty-one, Oscar Wilde died at forty-six, Chekhov at forty-four, Dylan Thomas at thirty-nine— let me repeat that, so no one thinks I've gone up on my lines. Chekhov died at forty-four. Forty-four! Also of tuberculosis. In his German country home, he, too, coughed up blood into a handkerchief – which I don't have – and the doctor was summoned and when he arrived, Chekhov, who spoke not a word of German, said, "Ich sterbe." "I am dying." So the doctor ordered champagne – which is apparently what one did in early-twentieth-century Germany when one's patient was at death's door – he ordered champagne. And when it arrived, the doctor poured him a glass, and Chekhov took a sip, and the great playwright said, in Russian, "I have not tasted champagne in a long time," and then he, too, lost consciousness, fell over, and died. A week later, when his funeral procession was making its way through the streets of Moscow, it crossed paths with the funeral procession of a Czarist general, led by a military band. Chekhov's mourners got momentarily disoriented and ended up following the band. When Chekhov's casket arrived at the cemetery, there was no one behind it. Chekhov was buried without an audience. I'd like to think that Chekhov – if he hadn't been in the casket at the time – would have appreciated the irony.

Pause.

He was buried next to his father.

Pause.

My father was cremated. He died at seventy-nine. Of congestive heart failure. There were a lot of things going on, but that's ultimately what got him: congestive heart failure. He led a good life. Seventy-eight and a half years of a good life. It wasn't until the last few months that things started to get funny. He started to hallucinate. He hallucinated, for instance, that every empty chair in his house was occupied by a stranger. He'd walk into the dining room, and there would be six people seated at the table ready to eat. None of whom he knew. He would walk into the living room to watch television, and there was someone in his recliner. He would wake up in the middle of the night and in the empty chair at the foot of his bed would be a stranger, staring back at him in the dark. My father stopped reading for the last six months of his life, because whenever he went back into his study, in his favorite reading chair was a stranger. We tried to convince my father that this wasn't so, but this was real for him.

> *Pause.*

August 8, 2008, I received a phone call from my brother. Or my sister-in-law. The events of that day are fuzzy, and I know it's an insignificant detail, but I want to make sure that everything I say tonight is absolutely true, so I think it was my brother, it may have been my sister-in-law. I answered the phone and he, or she, said, "Dad is not doing well. You should get up here as soon as possible." So, we jumped in the car. Me, the woman I love dearly, although not enough, or perhaps not well enough, a woman from whom within a few months I would separate, and our two kids. And we drove five and a half hours north, to a tiny hospital in a tiny town in the Adirondack Mountains, and when we pulled into the parking lot, I turned to our kids and I said, "Be forewarned. Grandpa's not in very good shape. He might not even recognize you." So as we entered the hospital, we walked down this long corridor. Actually, it couldn't have been long, it was a tiny hospital – anyway, I remember it as long – and up ahead to the left was a nurses' station. Sort of a curved desk, and a nurse behind, and she was wearing one of those World War II-era white nurse's caps. I know that can't be so, but I distinctly remember that. And she stood up and she said, "May I help you?" And I said, "We're looking for Willie Schmidt." And she said, with far more empathy than you can possibly imagine from the line she actually delivered, she said, "Oh. You're two minutes late. He's dead."

> *His knees buckle. Or, rather, he buckles his knees.*

So, we went into the hospital room and my father was, in fact, gone. Well, he wasn't gone, he was still there, but he was dead. That night we went back to what was now suddenly my mother's home, and I knew that I was going to have trouble falling asleep that night. In order to fall asleep most nights I need one of two things. I either need to have sex or I need to read a book. And for any number of reasons, sex was out that night. So, I went back into my father's study. He had three or four times as many books as I have. The only problem is they're all nonfiction. Literally, every single one of them. The only novel I ever remember my father reading was one of those Zane

Gray books. A dime western. Why he read that I have no idea. I mean, there was only one play of mine that he liked, because it was about historical characters. I remember the first full-length play I wrote, when I was about twenty-two or twenty-three, and I gave it to him to read. It was called "The Two-Headed Man." It was about a bearded lady in a traveling circus.

Pause.

Write what you know. And I gave that to my father to read, and the next day I said, "Dad, what did you think?" And he said, "I have to be honest. I didn't like it." "Really? Wow. Why?" He said, "Well, it just seemed made-up to me." I said, "Well, it is a play. It is sort of by definition made-up." And he said, "I know. That's what I didn't like about it." "So, you didn't like my work of fiction because it's not nonfiction." And he said, "Yes. I think that's right." "Jesus Christ, Dad, there's not much I can do about that." And then I remember having this argument – well, it wasn't so much an argument as it was a monologue, because I was the only one doing any of the talking. Like one of those college-dormitory diatribes about the value and the efficacy of art. Ya know, that this is what separates us from the other animals, that we create these narratives that might not necessarily be true, but somehow they help us arrive at a deeper, fuller truth, that we, ya know, as humans, we can see not only what is, but we can imagine what could be, what should be, what might – and, of course, my father's eyes were glazing over the whole time – so I pulled out my ace in the hole, which was a quote from Edward Albee – I was reading a lot of Albee at the time. I didn't tell him it was from Albee, I just pretended that this nugget of wisdom came off the top of my head, and I said, "But Dad, a play is fiction, and fiction is fact distilled into truth."

Pause.

And my father said – and I will never forget this – well, I will forget— eventually I'll forget everything, but of the things I forget last, hopefully this is one of them – my father turned to me and he said, "That is the most ridiculous thing I've ever heard."

Pause.

So this was the man whose books I was perusing that night for something, anything to help me fall asleep. I remember the one book he wrote was on the shelves – he actually co-wrote it, it was based on his doctoral dissertation, he was a scholar and a teacher of American History – it was called "North Carolinians in the Continental Congress." And there was another one on the shelf, that he had edited, called "American Naval Forces: 1750-1870." Three volumes. I mean, these books wouldn't put me to sleep, they'd bore me wide awake. In vain, I looked for something, anything to read, and suddenly one book, as books are wont to do, leapt off the shelves at me. It was …

Taking a copy off the shelf.

… Thornton Wilder's "Our Town." Now, for those of you who don't know "Our Town" – and I'm always shocked that not everyone knows "Our Town" – this is the great American play. And anyone who disagrees, I will drop the gloves and step outside right now. This is the real thing. It is wise and funny and true and unsentimental and formally inventive. A more sentimental man than I would say that there was a reason that this book was on my shelves that night. A cosmic reason. But I tend to think the explanation is more prosaic. This is my favorite play. I reread it every year or so. I'm sure a few summers before I'd brought it up, read it – I have several, well, I had several copies of it, I'm down to, I think, two now – and I probably read it and left it up there and my mother, not knowing what it was, shoved it back on my father's bookshelf, and that's how it got there.

Pause.

"Our Town" is set in the fictional town of Grover's Corners, New Hampshire, and it concerns primarily a young couple, George and Emily, who grow up next door to each other, fall in love, get married and raise a family. The first act is called "Daily Life," the second is called "Love and Marriage," and, as the Stage Manager says, "I reckon I don't have to tell you what the third act is about."

Pause.

That's what I decided to read the night of my father's death: Act Three of "Our Town." Let me just read you the stage directions at the beginning of Act Three so you get a sense.

Ed Schmidt

Holds the book at arm's length.

I have to hold it out here because of my eyes …

Reading.

"During the intermission the audience has seen the stagehands arranging the stage. On the right hand side, a little right of the center, ten or twelve ordinary chairs have been placed in three openly spaced rows facing the audience. These are graves in the cemetery." Now, we quickly discover that the latest entrant to the cemetery is Emily Webb, dead at twenty-seven, in childbirth. And she quickly discovers that she has the ability to relive her life, to relive the days of her life. The other dead people implore her not to. She insists. So they say, If you're going to, then choose an insignificant day. Choose the most insignificant day of your life; that will be significant enough. And so she chooses to relive her eleventh birthday. And with the Stage Manager beside her, she watches as her mother prepares breakfast, as her father returns from a trip to … New York State, as she and her brother prepare for school, and she is struck by the fact that no one really sees, truly sees, how fragile and precious and fleeting life really is, that they are living this insignificant day as if it were insignificant. And the pain of that revelation is so great that she decides to return to the land of the dead.

Pause.

It's the most heartbreaking scene in … in all of theater. And that's what I read. I don't know what I was looking for in Act Three of "Our Town" – wisdom or solace or truth or something – but what I found within five pages was something entirely different. I was completely and utterly bored. There was nothing more insignificant to my life at that time than the death of a fictional character in a fictional town in a work of fiction. I was in the midst of the real thing and I had turned to a fictionalization, an aestheticization of that thing. And I know that's what fiction does, but as I was reading this, I thought, I don't like this play. In fact, I hate it. And I hate it because it's not nonfiction. And I thought, Jesus Christ, he's dead four hours and already I've turned into my father. My mother, my grieving mother in the other room, could have used whatever shred of wisdom and solace I could have provided, and I needed the same from her, and instead, in my moment of greatest need, I had turned to a play.

And a play that suddenly made no sense to me. And I thought, if it makes no sense to read "Our Town" in my moment of greatest need, then it makes no sense to read "Our Town" at any time. And if it makes no sense to read "Our Town" at any time, then it makes no sense to read any play at any time. And if it makes no sense to read any play at any time, then it makes no sense to write any play at any time. And in that moment, I decided to walk away.

Pause.

Now, giving up the life of a playwright, as you can imagine, after thirty-two years was not easy. I mean, this is deep, deep in my bones. This is who I am. When people would ask me, "What do you do?" I would say, "I am a playwright." I cannot give that answer any more. I have for the last two-plus years not seen a play, I have not read a play, I have not written a line of dialogue. So giving up the life of a playwright was not easy. What has proved surprisingly easy is giving up the accoutrements of the life. Namely, the books.

Gesturing to the books.

I have, over those thirty-two years, amassed quite a library. It began at two thousand theater books, approximately. It's now down to about sixteen hundred. Five thousand different plays. Now, I'm asked this question every night. I was asked it last night. So, I've decided, from now on, to preemptively ask the question myself and answer it before anyone asks me. The question is this: Have you read them all? Well, the long answer is, if you started reading tomorrow – or let's say Monday, because this is going to be your job. Nine to five, five days a week, an hour for lunch, two weeks' vacation a year – you would finish in about seven and a half years. That's the long answer. The short answer is: Yes. In fact, I have read every single one of these plays. I know how pathetic that sounds. A more sentimental man than I would say that I did not waste those fifteen thousand hours, but I know the truth. I gave my life to these books, and they have not given me enough in return, and so I am giving them away.

Pause.

To you. And that is why you're here tonight.

Pause.

At the end of the evening, each of you will walk out the door with any one book off the shelves. The run of the play will end when all the books are gone, when the bookshelves are bare. That last, lonely night, when those last, lonely ten or twelve books go into your hands and out that door, and my divorce from the theater will be final.

Pause.

Now, when I first decided to get rid of these plays – because I did not buy them to have or to collect or to catalog; I bought these books for one reason and one reason alone: to read them to help me become a better playwright. And once I decided I was no longer a playwright, these books were suddenly of no value, of no worth, at all to me. They meant nothing. And so I had to get rid of them.

Pause.

My first thought was to give them away, to an institution, as a charitable contribution, sort of a magnanimous gesture, and what better place to give away my theater books than to the high school where I was first introduced to the theater: The Phillips Exeter Academy, in Exeter, New Hampshire, where I transferred my Junior and Senior years of high school. So I called the chair of the theater department at Exeter. I'd not been back in over two decades. I said, "I have two thousand theater books, five thousand plays, that I'm getting rid of. Would you be interested in taking them off my hands?" And she said, "Yes, absolutely. How much would that cost us?" I said, "Nothing. I'm giving them away for free." She said, "That's wonderful." I said, "I'm going to be up in New Hampshire in three weeks, how about I drop by, we have a little chat, have some coffee, we work out the details?" She said, "That's wond— in fact, better yet, let's instead, because this is such a lovely gesture on your part, let's invite all of the theater students, all of the theater facul— no, even better than that, let's invite all of the students and all of the faculty, and you can give a presentation. It'll be an event. We'll hold it in the theater. You can talk about your collection and why you're giving it away to Exeter and what the school meant to you." And I thought, That's fantastic. An excuse to get back onstage one more time.

Pause.

So, for the next three weeks I put together this PowerPoint presentation, with photos of the books, and charts and graphs and photos of old productions of mine, and stories about the books. I had it whittled down to an airtight ninety minutes.

Pause.

Three weeks later, I set off northeast, towards Exeter, New Hampshire, in my car, and about halfway there was hit by a massive blizzard, but I was not going to be deterred. I drove through the snowstorm and eventually made it to the campus at 6:45. My presentation was scheduled to begin at 7 o'clock. I pulled up, I threw the car into park, and I jumped out with my laptop under my arm and I raced across campus, and I got there at about five of seven, and as I approached the doors of the theater building, these grand, wooden doors, the same doors through which I had passed twenty-five, thirty years earlier, I spotted, on the left-hand door, a sign. A small, handwritten sign – it wasn't even eight-and-a-half by eleven, it was like five by seven – and it said: "Tonight. 7:00 – 7:30. Ed Schmidt talks about his books."

Pause.

My first thought was: 7:00 to 7:30!? There's no way I'm going to do this in a half hour. And my second thought was: they have no marketing budget. Because this is the best they can do? So I walked through the doors, into the building, through the lobby, not knowing what to expect when I got into the theater itself, and I pushed the doors open … there were two people in the audience. The chair of the theater department and the husband of one of the teachers who was gone for the weekend. No other faculty, no students. And I know that I had decided that these books were worthless, meaningless, valueless to me, but I thought, I will be goddamned if I'm gonna give them away to people who think they are equally worthless and meaningless and valueless. I know that doesn't make any sense, but I thought, if I'm going to give these books away, they have to be to people who are as passionate and as obsessive about them as I once was. So, we had a quick chat, I said, "There's probably no need for me to do the ninety-minute PowerPoint," and she said, "That's probably right." And so we discussed a few things and we shook hands, and I got in my car and drove all the way back to Brooklyn. Three days later, I emailed her. I said, "I've had second thoughts. I think I'm going to do something else with the books."

Pause.

Because as I walked out of the theater that night, after my non-presentation, into the lobby, tall, soaring lobby – the walls lined with posters from past productions at the school – I spotted, in the far left corner, the poster from the first play that I was ever in. "Pygmalion," by George Bernard Shaw.

Pause.

Now, when I was in high school, I was a jock. I played soccer in the fall, basketball in the winter, and I ran track in the spring. That was my best sport. I was All-State in track. And the track coach was thrilled to have me there. I was going to anchor his track team for the next two years. And as spring approached, he approached me every day and told me how excited he was about the upcoming track season. I, however, had a different plan. Because I had fallen in love, from afar, with a girl named Lizza Clifford. Lizza was tall and willowy and blonde, and she had a ponytail out the back of her baseball cap, and she grew up on a farm in Maine. She was every cliché in the book, and I had read that book over and over and over. Now, I was so shy, I had never kissed a girl before, so I hadn't spoken to Lizza, much less asked her out. So here was my plan. She was widely considered the finest actor on campus. She was a Senior, she'd been accepted early decision to Yale to study drama, she was going to be an actress. So, rather than run track that spring, I was going to try out for the spring play, "Pygmalion." I was going to be cast as Henry Higgins, Lizza would be Eliza Doolittle, we would meet, we would fall in love, and we'd live happily ever after. It was foolproof.

Pause.

I had no worries about the audition. I had a sort of athlete's confidence about me, and my voice was deeper than every other boy's who was auditioning, and also my English accents were vast and impeccable. I had seen nearly every episode of "Monty Python," so I knew I'd be fine there. I read for Henry Higgins and I just killed. I was brilliant. I knew I had the role. The next morning, the cast list went up on those doors to the theater, and I rushed from my dorm, down to the theater, and I rushed up to the doors and my first surprise was that Henry Higgins had not been cast with Ed Schmidt. They had given the role instead to a boy from England. My second surprise was that Lizza Clifford was not Eliza Doolittle. They had given the role to a girl named Kitty … I can't remember her last name … Kitty something. She was a lovely girl, she was a musical-theater performer, beautiful voice, but she was anything but a kitty. She was about four-foot-two by about five-foot-two. She was ovoid. And I thought, Oh, my god, they've given it to Kitty instead of Lizza! That makes no sense! And I scanned the rest of the cast list, and there at the bottom was my name, next to Freddy Eynsford-Hill. Freddy is the gentleman caller, the nerdy gentleman caller, who falls madly in love with Eliza and, for God knows what reason, she decides to marry him at the end of the play. And my final surprise of the day was that Lizza Clifford's name was nowhere to be found. I found out later that afternoon that Lizza, because she was going to spend the rest of her life onstage, had decided that spring semester of her Senior year that she was going to try something new. She had decided to join the track team.

Pause.

So, the first day of rehearsals – this was all new to me – we did a read-through around a big rectangular table and, I have to confess, I had not read the play all the way through. I had only read my sides for Henry Higgins because I knew that was the role I was going to get, so I was more than a little surprised to discover that, late in Act Five, there is a scene underneath a lamppost in which Freddy and Eliza kiss. And when the director read that stage direction – "Freddy and Eliza kiss" – the entire cast broke out into laughter. Ha ha ha, Ed and Kitty are going to have to kiss. And I thought, Oh my God – and believe me, when I was sixteen I was no great shakes. I was one of those kids whose nose and ears grow much faster than the rest of their face. It took, like, two years for my face to catch up to my nose. It's still got a few more years to catch up to my ears. It would take decades before I turned into that "sturdy, pleasant-looking man" that the New York *Times* so generously describes me as.

Pause.

So, as I was looking at Kitty, I was thinking, Oh, my God, I'm gonna have to kiss Kitty! And I'm sure she was thinking, Oh, my God, I'm gonna have to kiss the kid with the ears and the nose! And the director pulled us aside after the read-through, and he said, "I know. The kiss. Everybody laughed. But, listen, here's the most important thing: don't worry. Don't worry about the kiss. Just don't worry. It's late in Act Five. It's not even a scene we're going to rehearse in the next five weeks, it's a six-week rehearsal period, we'll get to it late, and it's going to be simple. It's a quick, choreographed scene, it's like a dance. It'll take us ten seconds to do. So don't worry. Don't worry. Don't—" The more he said: "Don't worry," of course, the more I worried.

Pause.

So, as rehearsals progressed— no, I remember, the first rehearsal. The first rehearsal we did theater games. Again, completely new to me. The theater game was: we were all assigned an inanimate object. I was a rock. And the twenty or twenty-five of us in the cast were onstage and the director would blow a whistle and we would amble amongst each other and he would blow the whistle again and we would turn and face our nearest fellow castmate and and and and … express our … inanimateness to each other.

Pause.

There was one kid in the cast who was in my dorm, though I'd never formally met him, his name was Rory Calhoun. He was an odd kid. And he seemed, through this whole exercise, he seemed to be stalking me. I'd turn around and I'd see him approach and he'd brush past me and out of the side of his mouth – because we were supposed to be silent, we were inanimate objects … why we were moving I'm not quite sure – and he'd brush past me and out of the side of his mouth he'd whisper, "This is bullshit. This is bullshit." And I'd turn around and he'd be gone, and I'd come over here and he'd pass by me this way, and he'd go, "This is bullshit, this is bullshit." And the whistle would blow, and invariably I'd— Rory was a fork! I just remembered that! Invariably I'd turn and there would be Rory, and I was trying to do the right thing and and and … be a rock, and Rory, instead of being a fork, he'd whisper, "This is bullshit. Complete and utter bullshit." And I thought, He's absolutely right! This is bullshit. I like this kid, I like his attitude, I'm going to be friends with Rory Calhoun. In fact, to this day, we are friends. It's the one good thing that came out of that production.

Pause.

So, as rehearsals progressed, week after week after week, we never got to the kiss. Finally, dress rehearsal is coming up, morning of dress rehearsal, the director pulls Kitty and me aside, and he says, "Let's go over the kiss now. We'll explain it quickly and then, tonight, during dress rehearsal, you'll do the kiss for real." So, here's how it went.

Acting out the choreography.

He said, "Ed, you lean into Kitty like this. And Kitty, with your right hand, put it on Ed's left cheek." And then I was meant to turn away, and with her left hand on my right cheek, she would turn me back and gently pull me towards her and we would kiss. Just like that. One, two, three. We'll do it tonight at dress rehearsal.

Pause.

Now, anyone who's ever been involved in the theater knows that dress rehearsals are notoriously disastrous. What should have taken two hours took more than seven hours, and since this scene was late in Act Five, we never got to the kiss. My first ever kiss was going to happen onstage, with Kitty, in front of all my buddies from the soccer and basketball teams. I was terrified.

Pause.

So, opening night, of four performances, opening night, I had a few scenes in the first couple acts, and I did well. The accent got laughs, so I was confident coming into the final scene. But as I approached Kitty, she was standing under the lamppost, I suddenly froze. My mind went blank. I couldn't remember what to do. And Kitty, praise Jesus, she sensed my panic, she was an old pro, and …

Acting it out.

… she reached her right hand towards me, and suddenly it all snapped back into place, and I moved towards her and I leaned in, and she put her right hand on my left cheek, and I turned away, and she put her left hand on my right cheek, and she pulled me gently towards her and our lips met and ... Kitty had the softest, most succulent lips you can possibly imagine. This rush of testosterone coursed through me ...

Still acting it out, with rocket-launch sound effects.

... from my toes to my fingertips, and I got an instant erection. Enormous! Well, relatively speaking, enormous erection. And instinctively, I put both my hands on my crotch and pulled back and held the kiss and the audience roared with laughter. They thought it was hilarious. The director pulled us aside after the performance and he said, "Ed, that was brilliant! Brilliant acting!" Little did he know, I wasn't acting at all. I just had no control of my genitals. So, for the next three nights, the exact same thing happened. I would lean in, the right hand on my left cheek, the turn away, the left hand on my right cheek, the kiss, the erection, the hands on the crotch, hold the kiss, the A-frame, and every night we brought the house down. At the end of the four-night run, I was considered the finest comic actor at Phillips Exeter Academy. It was my new identity.

Pause.

After the last performance, we had a cast party. An open cast party. Again, all new to me. And Lizza Clifford showed up, I remember. With her new boyfriend. From the track team. But I didn't care. Because in those last four days, I had fallen in love with Kitty. And as the party started to break up, I worked up all my courage, and I approached Kitty and I said, "May I walk you back to your dorm tonight?" And she said, "That would be lovely." And so we walked back. It was a beautiful May evening in New England – the stars were out, a light breeze – I so desperately wanted to hold her hand. But I was scared. So we walked side by side, along the path, and I walked her all the way back, and there was the door to her dormitory, and steps leading up to the door, and a light above, just like in the lamppost scene, and Kitty walked up three or four steps, so she was almost eye level with me, and I said, very gentlemanly, "Kitty, may I kiss you goodnight?" And she said, "You may not." "Why?" "Because I have a boyfriend back home in Massachusetts and we're going to get married after we graduate from college." And then I said the rashest, most ill-considered words I've ever spoken. I said, "But, Kitty, I love you. And I know you love me, too." And she said, "What in God's name gave you that idea?" "The kiss!" I said. "The kiss!" And Kitty, God bless her, she was seventeen years old, she said, "My good man, that was a stage kiss." And she turned on her heel and she opened the door and she walked into her dormitory and she let the door close behind her.

Pause.

I was crushed.

Pause.

I trudged all the way back to the theater to pick up my backpack so that I could go back to my dorm and just die. And as I walked into the theater, there were only five or six people – Rory was still there, I remember, sitting on the side of the stage, and his legs were dangling over, and I walked up and sat next to Rory and I spilled my guts. I told him that I'd never kissed a girl before, that I'd fallen madly in love with Lizza, and she had a boyfriend, and I'd fallen madly in love with Kitty, and she had a boyfriend, and my life was over. I'm not ashamed to say that I wept on Rory Calhoun's shoulder that night.

Not a terrible French accent.

"Sometimes ze stage tears are real." And Rory was a cynical kid, but he was there in my moment of greatest need. And I remember, at one point he put his arm around my shoulder, and it took me a good hour, an hour and a half, to tell him the story of my life, and when I was finally done and had dried my tears, we stood up to walk back to our dorm, and we were the only people left in the theater – just the ghost light was on – and as we walked across the stage, with Rory leading the way, towards the side exit, which would lead us down the path to our dormitory, Rory, halfway across, stopped. And he turned to me. And, I swear to God …

Acting it out.

… he reached out with his right hand and he touched my left cheek, and I turned away, and he reached out with his left hand and he put it on the back of my neck, and he pulled me towards him, and our lips touched, and we kissed. I didn't get an erection, at least not right away. It was a full, fifteen, twenty-minute make-out session. My first ever real kiss happened onstage, in the glow of a ghost light, with Rory Calhoun.

Pause.

As I say, we are friends to this day, Rory and I. And neither one of us has ever mentioned that incident since.

Pause.

So as I walked out of the theater, into the lobby, with the chair of the theater department and the husband of one of the teachers who was gone for the weekend, I saw that poster – "Pygmalion" – and I thought, I have that book back home. There is a story attached to that book. There are stories attached to so many of my books. Rather than give them away to people who don't want them – for free – why don't I write something, about the books, and give them away to people who do want them? And maybe make twenty dollars a head in the process. Which is what has brought us all here, together, this evening.

Pause.

In a few minutes, I am going to call an intermission. I will turn the lights on. Feel free to roam through the bookcases. Ten, fifteen minutes, choose any book you would like. We will gather again briefly, I will stamp them, record the date, maybe talk about them a little bit, and then you will be on your way, and I will be …

Counting the number of people in the audience; let's say, ten.

… ten books closer to the end.

Pause.

So. Before we get to the intermission. A quick overview of the books I have. As I said, I started with two thousand. I am now …

This number, of course, was different for each performance.

… four hundred and thirty are gone.

A guided tour of the bookshelves.

This entire wall, as well as that small wall, and about half of those books over there, are all plays by single playwrights. I don't mean unmarried. I mean one playwright per book. So, it's either a single play or it's a collection of plays written by one playwright. They're arranged alphabetically. At least they were. They've gotten a little mixed up, but they're roughly alphabetical. It used to be "Friends," by Kobo Abe, that was the first play, it's now "Green Julia," by Paul Abelman. It winds around – there's Edward Albee and Brecht and Horton Foote and Christopher Hampton and George S. Kaufman, and over there is Molière and Odets and O'Neill and on and on, and over here is Shakespeare and Shaw and Wilder and Williams, and the last play in alphabetical order is "Ladies at the Alamo," by Paul Zindel.

Next section.

These two rows down here, as well as, roughly, these three columns, are all collections of plays. They've been anthologized by their editors in various ways and organized accordingly by me. This is the foreign section here. There's English, Irish, French, German, Italian, Norwegian, Belgian – who knew? – Czech, Australian, Latin American, Arabic, Japanese, Chinese, African, South African, East African – it's like the United Nations.

Bottom row.

The bottom row is mostly full-length plays, collections of those. These plays here are organized by theater company, these by alma mater – there are Harvard and Yale plays.

Another section.

Oh, these plays here! I organized this section for my own amusement – this book is called "Modern Plays," this is "A Book of Modern Plays," that's "Modern One-Act Plays," "Modern American Plays," "Modern American Drama," "Modern Drama in America," "Contemporary American Drama," "Contemporary American Plays,"

Ed Schmidt

"New American Plays," "New American Theater," "New Theater in America," and the book that was taken last night, right in here, was called "New and Contemporary Drama in America." So, if you're interested in new, contemporary, modern American plays, right here.

Two columns.

These two columns, roughly, are nonfiction. Theory, criticism, history, autobiography, biography, letters. So, if you're of a more pedantic bent, this might be where you'll want to start.

On the top of the bookcases.

The books on top of the bookcases are series of plays. I'd like to say I have complete series. I used to. This was a twenty-volume series, "The Drama," from 1904, fantastic old books. I checked online; the going rate for a complete set of "The Drama": two thousand dollars. It stayed intact for a long time – I don't think anyone wanted to the first one – and then suddenly someone took volume six, last week, and instantly devalued the series by about fifteen hundred dollars. This is "America's Lost Plays," twenty volumes – if you read them, you'll quickly discover why they were lost. Someone took volumes three and four a few weeks ago. Over here there's the "Best One Act Plays" series. I have a lot of one-act plays.

Another section.

The ten or so books over here are the how-to playwriting section. So, if anyone wants to follow in my illustrious footsteps, there's plenty of useless information here.

Pause.

Let's see, what else?

Pause.

What's gone?

Pause.

Oh! The last play –it used to be a play by Howard Zinn, the historian, he wrote a play called "Emma," about Emma Goldman, that one's gone. Let's see, last night. What went last night? Um … let me see if I can remember … "New and Contemporary Drama in America." "Ulysses in Nighttown." Lee Breuer's "Gospel at Colonus." A collection of Camus plays. Collection of Horton Foote plays. Garcia Lorca's "The Public and Play Without a Title." "Luv," by Murray Schisgal. Um … oh! A weird collection. "13 Plays of Crime and Detection." A copy of "Our Town." An Edward Sheldon play. Can't repeat the title. And a how-to book. Called … "The Drama: Its Laws and Technique," I think.

Pause.

Anyway, as I say, there are still over fifteen hundred books. I think this search will be more about possibility for all of you than anything.

Pause.

I will be in and out for most of this intermission. Look around, wander, browse, make yourselves at home. If you have any questions, you can certainly ask me. If you're looking for a specific play or a specific playwright and you can't find it in the alphabetical section, I might be able to find it in one of the collections.

Pause.

So. That's the lay of the land. Before we go to intermission, does anyone have any questions? About the books, about the logistics of intermission, about anything. Any questions from anyone?

Audience members either ask questions or don't.

OK. We are almost at the end of Act One. These are the last lines of Act One of "My Last Play."

Pause. Gathers himself. Delivers the final lines of Act One of "Our Town."

Ed Schmidt

"That's the end of the first act, friends. You can go and smoke now, those that smoke."

He bows and exits upstairs.

End of Act One

ACT TWO

During intermission, audience members browse the bookshelves. ED SCHMIDT *appears once or twice and answers questions, makes suggestions, helps locate plays, engages in conversation. After each audience member has chosen a book,* ED SCHMIDT *suggests that the chairs be arranged in a circle, "sort of like a book club!" He asks the audience members to pass the books to him, so that he can stamp and date them. He has a custom-made stamp that reads "My Last Play," an inkpad, a pen, and an index card on which to record the title and author of each book.*

During Act Two, ED SCHMIDT *will comment on each book, stamp it, date it, and pass it back to its new owner. Act Two is meant to feel conversational, casual, unscripted.*

There are two kinds of responses to books that audience members have chosen: improvised and scripted. Unbeknownst to the audience, five of the stories are scripted; minor details are altered to make those stories more believable and consistent. All the other interactions are improvised.

The five scripted stories, which are part of every performance, are, in order: 1) the Williamstown bookstore story, which must involve an American playwright whose plays were published in the 1970s or early 1980s (in this performance, it is David Mamet); 2) the "Leave a mark" story, which must involve a famous playwright, actor, or director who was alive during the last thirty years (in this performance, it is Peter Brook); 3) the Strand bookstore story, which could be any book; 4) the one-day-playwriting-class story, which must involve an English-speaking playwright who was alive in the late 1980s (in this performance, it is Edward Albee); and 5) the book-my-father-gave-me story, which could be any book (in this performance, it is a book withdrawn from the Asheville Public Library; on a few occasions, an audience member chose a book that had actually been inscribed to ED SCHMIDT *by his father).* ED SCHMIDT *organizes the books so that he can tell these five stories in order.*

What follows is a near-verbatim transcript of Act Two of the February 24, 2011, performance, which ten people attended.

ED SCHMIDT

It's only ... ten, right?

He counts the books aloud.

OK, as I said, my memory's fading, so I'm going to write the titles as we go, so I have a list of what books have gone. Let's see. Viola Spolin. *Improvisation for the Theater.* Who chose this?

AUDIENCE MEMBER 1

I did.

ED SCHMIDT

You did. And why is that?

AUDIENCE MEMBER 1

Well, I'm teaching acting now, so.

ED SCHMIDT

Oh. OK. Where?

AUDIENCE MEMBER 1

In New Jersey.

ED SCHMIDT

Where in New Jersey?

AUDIENCE MEMBER 1

East Brunswick.

ED SCHMIDT

OK.

AUDIENCE MEMBER 1

The Acting Academy.

ED SCHMIDT

I have to confess, I know I read this, years ago, when I was briefly contemplating a career as an actor, but I don't remember a thing about it. But, if memory serves, it's considered one of the classic texts on improvisation.

AUDIENCE MEMBER 1

Yes.

ED SCHMIDT

OK. Good. So this choice is practical!

AUDIENCE MEMBER 1

It certainly is.

ED SCHMIDT

Great. It'll be put to good use. Let me stamp it ...

Stamps and dates the book, hands it back.

There you go.

AUDIENCE MEMBER 1

Thank you.

ED SCHMIDT

You're welcome.

He records the author and title on the index card. Next book.

"Romeo and Juliet." Who chose this?

AUDIENCE MEMBER 2

I did.

ED SCHMIDT

And why is that?

AUDIENCE MEMBER 2

Because it's a classic?

ED SCHMIDT

It is a classic. That is true. Why this particular classic, rather than any of the other classics?

3 Plays

AUDIENCE MEMBER 2

Because … I'm not an old person, but the letters are bigger.

ED SCHMIDT

The letters are bigger! OK. You'll appreciate this in your old age.

Opening the book, considering it.

I actually remember where I bought this book. In Stratford, Ontario. One of the, I don't know, half dozen used bookstores in town. We used to go up every year to the Stratford Festival and then over to the Shaw Festival, in Niagara-on-the-Lake. We'd drive up from Brooklyn, get a spot at one of the campgrounds in the area, bring a tent, then every morning we'd line up at the box office for rush tickets and see two plays. A matinee and an evening performance. Very, very fond memories of those trips. I remember seeing Brian Bedford there for the first time. And Victor Garber. Brian Bedford starred in … "Coriolanus." Amazing actor.

As he stamps and dates the book.

Not that I'm advocating reading plays, but, if you feel so compelled, you can't go wrong with Shakespeare. And you can do far worse than "Romeo and Juliet."

He hands back the book, records the author and title on the index card.

AUDIENCE MEMBER 2

Thank you.

ED SCHMIDT

You're welcome. Next. I saw a Mamet here. "Speed-the-Plow." Who was that?

AUDIENCE MEMBER 3 *raises his hand.*

That was you. And why "Speed-the-Plow"?

AUDIENCE MEMBER 3

I've not read it, and I always thought Mamet spoke specially to me.

ED SCHMIDT

Really?

AUDIENCE MEMBER 3

Yes.

ED SCHMIDT

He spoke specially to me, too. This is the Madonna play. I remember seeing Madonna in the original Broadway production. At the … Booth, maybe? Are there any Mamet plays that you particularly like?

AUDIENCE MEMBER 3

I love "Glengarry." And "American Buffalo."

ED SCHMIDT

Same with me. And I'd add "Sexual Perversity" and … "Edmond," which I like a lot. Quick story about Mamet. As I said, when I was sixteen, I wrote my first play. About my failed love affair with Kitty. It was dreadful. Kind of derivative of Shaw, of all people, one-act, painfully maudlin. So, I didn't even think about getting involved in the theater again until my Junior year of college. I took a Theater 101 class – I have no idea why – and we had to do this end-of-semester original, creative project. Write a play or direct a scene or act in— I remember, I was building a set for … I can't remember which play … because I was kind of no longer interested in the theater and I was trying to doing the easiest thing I could think of. And in the middle of one of these classes – about forty people in the class – one guy, a student, suddenly stands up, in the middle of the professor's speech, and he goes, at the top of his lungs, "Fuckin' Ruthie! Fuckin' Ruthie! Fuckin' Ruthie! Fuckin' Ruthie! Fuckin' Ruthie!" Five times, and I was like, "Jesus Christ, what the hell is going on?" and the professor didn't seem to be bothered by this interruption or anything, and then another guy stands up and he goes, "What?" As if he hadn't heard, as if this other guy hadn't said "Fuckin' Ruthie!" loud enough. So again, for the sixth time, he goes, "Fuckin' Ruthie!" And I thought, These people are crazy! It took me – I wasn't very bright – it took me a minute or so to realize, Oh, it's a scene from a play! It's their creative project! And it was "American Buffalo," by David Mamet. It was riveting! I was so energized by this mini-performance that, right after class, I thought, I have to read this play. Immediately. So I rushed down to the college bookstore, Renzi's, Renzi's Books – because I knew the library only had Shakespeare and Ibsen and Chekhov and all the old plays; they didn't have any contemporary plays – and I ran down and there was one bookshelf, about seventy books, of contemporary American plays, and there was "American Buffalo," and I pulled it off the shelf and I paid my … I think it was seven dollars, six ninety-nine, I ran back to my dormitory, I read it, it took me about ninety minutes, and I loved it, I was blown away by it, and I thought, I have to read every play David Mamet has ever written, every play on that bookshelf, but, ya know, they cost seven dollars each, and I don't have that kind of money, and also I'd read the play, I'd finished it, it took me an hour and a half, I didn't know what to do with it, I'm done – with a novel, you spend weeks reading it, but this took me an afternoon, not even – so the next day I returned to the bookstore and there was another Mamet play – "Lakeboat," I think – and I pulled it off the shelves, it was winter, I was wearing a big down jacket, and without anyone seeing I slipped it under my jacket and I walked out of the store. I went back to my dorm and, very carefully, without breaking the spine, I read "Lakeboat." Which took me about seventy minutes. And I loved that play, too. So, the next day, I went back to Renzi's, and, when no one was looking, I pulled out "Lakeboat" and I put it back onto the shelves and I took "Sexual Perversity in Chicago" and I slipped it under my jacket and I went back to my dorm and read that, and the next day I returned to the bookstore and exchanged "Sexual Perversity" for, I don't know, "Edmond," maybe, and I read that, and I read all of Mamet that way, and then I backed up and I started to read every book on that shelf, left to right, alphabetically – Albee and Durang and Horton Foote and Maria Irene Fornes and Gurney and Horowitz and Rochelle Owens and right down the line. And every day I'd put one book back and steal the … yeah, I stole it, I stole the next book and I'd read it and bring it back and steal another and I almost got through the entire row of books. It was Lanford Wilson's "Fifth of July" that tripped me up. As I was walking out the door, with that play under my jacket, I felt a hand on my shoulder. It was Mr. Renzi. The owner. Mr. Renzi was the father-in-law of John Sayles, the screenwriter and director and novelist. His daughter, Maggie, who was a dancer and a choreographer, was married to Sayles. Mr. Renzi led me upstairs into a little room, his office. I tried to explain, he didn't want to hear it. He walked out of the room and he closed the door. And he called the cops. Williamstown's finest. One guy. He opened the door, he sat down, and he started to ask me questions. And I tried to explain. That I wasn't really stealing the book, that I was going to read it and bring it back tomorrow, that I'd done the same with, like, sixty or seventy books in the store – oh, I shouldn't've said that! – but I brought them all back, and none the worse for the wear. He didn't believe me. I said, "It's true, you can quiz me! From Albee to Wilson, I know them all!" I've read them all. I don't keep them, I don't ruin them, I don't mark them up. I just can't afford to buy them. And they still didn't believe me. And Mr. Renzi, at one point – he was a really nice guy, kind of gruff, but beloved, in the way that gruff old men are beloved, he was a legend in town – and at one point, his eyes started to well up. He was heartbroken by this. And he turned to me and he asked, "Why do you think it's ok for you to steal my books?" I was going to offer the "I didn't really steal them" defense, but I'd already tried that and it hadn't worked, so – and I hesitate to say this, because it's going to make me sound even more pretentious than I am (and, believe me, I'm really pretentious) – so I said: "Because. I am. An artist." And the instant the words came out of my mouth, I thought, God, you're an asshole. "Because I am an artist." So the cop and Mr. Renzi left the room and they talked for a few minutes and the cop came back into the office and he said, "Mr. Renzi has decided to drop the charges against you. But," he said, "under one condition. That you never set foot in his bookstore again." Which broke my heart. Because it was the only good bookstore in town. But I had no choice. And he wasn't going to press charges. I don't know exactly why Mr. Renzi— I think I must have touched a nerve? His daughter was a dancer, his son-in-law was a writer, he owned the bookstore, and he also owned the movie theater in town. So maybe "I am an artist" somehow, for some reason, touched him. Moved him. Ya know, convinced him that, maybe, what I'd done was, if not justified or even legal, then maybe it was in some way … I don't know, understandable. That was the closest I've ever come to incarceration. So …

To AUDIENCE MEMBER 3, *as he stamps and dates the book.*

... a word of advice: if you're ever pulled over by the cops – for speeding, or jaywalking, or assault with a deadly weapon, whatever – I can't guarantee anything, but it's worth a try. Just say, "But Officer, I am an artist." It worked for me.

Handing the book to AUDIENCE MEMBER 3.

There you go.

He records the author and title on the index card.

I went back to the school for a reunion – two, three years ago – and the bookstore is no longer a bookstore. Mr. Renzi, I don't know – sold it? died? – I don't know. It's now a sandwich shop. And I couldn't even bring myself to go in and order lunch.

On to the next book.

Let's see. "Kindness," by Adam Rapp.

To AUDIENCE MEMBER 4.

You chose this. You actually asked me to help you choose between two Adam Rapp plays. What do you know of Adam Rapp?

AUDIENCE MEMBER 4

I met him a couple months ago working a benefit for a theater company. He was a really interesting person and I'd never read his work. I read a lot of plays, but – I have a similar collection; I'm one of those hopeless aspiring playwrights ...

ED SCHMIDT

Join the crowd.

AUDIENCE MEMBER 4

But I've been eating up his plays lately. I've read six in the last month and a half, and you have two that I don't have.

ED SCHMIDT

Yes. Well. OK. I don't want to influence you one way or the other. You like them?

AUDIENCE MEMBER 4

I do.

ED SCHMIDT

Stamping and recording the date.

Good. I've read a few. I'll leave it at that.

Hands the book back.

And he's a nice guy? I've never met him.

AUDIENCE MEMBER 4

Yes.

ED SCHMIDT

Well, that counts for something.

Records the author and title on the index card. Next book.

Let's see. Oh! Peter Brook. "The Empty Space." Who chose this?

AUDIENCE MEMBER 5

That was me.

ED SCHMIDT

That was you. OK. And why Peter Brook's "The Empty Space?"

AUDIENCE MEMBER 5

Well. Um. I was told to read it. And I accrued several late fees from the library, and I never cracked it. So.

ED SCHMIDT

You haven't read a word of it?

AUDIENCE MEMBER 5

No.

ED SCHMIDT

Are you involved in the theater?

AUDIENCE MEMBER 5

Yeah. I'm an actor.

ED SCHMIDT

I'm sorry to hear that.

AUDIENCE MEMBER 4

Stage whisper.

She's amazing!

ED SCHMIDT

Is she? Well. This is kind of the Holy Grail. This is the Bible.

Paging through it.

All of my underlines.

Ed Schmidt

AUDIENCE MEMBER 5

I know!

ED SCHMIDT

Oh, I wouldn't get too excited. I'm sure I underlined all the wrong stuff. Yeah. Wow. It's gonna be hard letting this one go. But I can always get it out of the library. If you ever return it. It's brilliant. Brilliant. So far ahead of its time. It's still so relevant and …

Reading the first sentences of the book.

"I can take any empty space and call it a bare stage. A man walks across this empty space whilst someone else is watching him, and this is all that is needed for an act of theatre to be engaged." That's it. That's the perfect description of theater, right there.

A deep breath to deal with giving this one away.

Have you seen any of his work?

AUDIENCE MEMBER 5

No.

ED SCHMIDT

I met him, I actually met him, briefly, when he was directing "The Mahabarata," at BAM. Years ago.

Re: the book.

And it's falling apart, which makes it even better. I went up to him at intermission, because I saw him in the back of the theater, in a corner, sort of hiding, all by himself, and, just like with Kitty, I screwed my courage to the sticking place and I walked up to him to introduce myself and I said, "Mr. Brook, I'm an aspiring playwright. Do you have any advice for me?" And he said – it was very cryptic, I still don't know exactly what he meant – but he said, "Leave a mark, son. Leave a mark." I'm not sure this is the kind of mark he meant ...

Stamping the book and recording the date.

... but it's the best I can do.

He hands the book to AUDIENCE MEMBER 5. *Records the author and title on the index card. Next book.*

Next ... "Vatzlav," by Mrozek.

AUDIENCE MEMBER 6

That's me.

ED SCHMIDT

That's you. Do you know his work?

AUDIENCE MEMBER 6

I'm Polish.

ED SCHMIDT

OK.

AUDIENCE MEMBER 6

So that's why I chose him. My mom is very fond of him.

ED SCHMIDT

This is great. He's great. Was great. Do you know this play?

AUDIENCE MEMBER 6

No.

ED SCHMIDT

I like this play. Very much. And a one-act, "At Sea," that's also really good. Absurdist, very much of its time. Slawomir Mrozek. 19 … 71, I think?

Checks the date of first production.

'70. Crazy play. Tons of scenes. They're on an island? There's a couple with a grown son who's a … bear, I think. And he wears diapers.

Paging through it.

Right. Oedipus Rex is a character. And the playwright himself. Very '70s idea. There was also another Polish guy, director … what's his name? Um … goddammit, I'll think of it.

AUDIENCE MEMBER 9

Grotowski.

ED SCHMIDT

No. He used to come to LaMama … Kantor! Tadeusz Kantor. One of the great unsung, unknown – in America, at least – geniuses of the theater. Those productions, when I was just out of college, they … anyway. Another story.

Looking at the book.

I remember where I bought this. You know how that happens sometimes? You might not remember everything about a book, but you can remember every detail of where you bought it? Where and when and what happened? I bought this at the Strand. Broadway and 12th. I used to work at the Strand. Has anybody – I always run into people who've worked at the Strand – has anybody here ever worked at the Strand?

No.

No.

Or, if someone has: "Then you'll know exactly what I'm talking about."

It was, without a doubt, the worst job of my life. Like working in a Soviet gulag. Utterly dehumanizing. I worked downstairs with all the reviewer's copies. It was terrible. But the great thing was – this was mid-eighties – we got paid in cash. It was all under the table. And the one thing that kept me working there – I lasted only four months – was that every Friday we were each allowed to buy six books – any six books – at half price. And we were all obsessive about books.

Re: the book. As he stamps and dates it.

And I remember: this was one of those half-price Friday books. I had read his collection of one-acts, so I figured, half price, why not? It was so weird. Absolutely cutthroat. We'd plan our Friday purchases days in advance. You'd see a book on, like, Tuesday and you'd think, I want this, but secretly, you wouldn't tell anyone, because then they might want that book, so you'd pull it off the shelf and hide it, in the … I don't know … the poetry section, because God forbid the customers actually found what they were looking for. But then it turns out you hadn't been sly enough, because another employee had seen you, and he decided he wanted that book, and he'd watch you hide it and he'd sneak around on, like, Wednesday, and grab it and hide it in the Philosophy section. And then, ya know, on Thursday, you'd be helping a customer find something by Kierkegaard and, holy shit!, there's your book! And so you'd snag it and hide it in the, whatever, the Cookbook section. It was high-level intrigue. So on Friday, right after the store closed, you'd race around to all your hiding places and gather your six books and take them to the front. That's when I really started to expand my theater-book collection, six books at a time. So, when I first decided to get rid of my books, my first thought, honestly, was not to give them away but to sell them. I didn't want to sell them on eBay, because, one at a time, that would take years. I wanted to sell them as a collection. So I called the Strand – the one place I knew that would buy a bunch of books, and I still knew a few people who worked there – I said, "I have this collection, two thousand theater books, would you be interested? Who do I contact? How do I go about it?" And there was a long pause. I remember him putting me on hold for … at least five minutes, and he came back and he said, "We can send an assessor out there this weekend to take a look at the collection." I said, "That would be great." So that Sunday, guy shows up at the door, he's about six foot four, shaved head, goatee, tattoos all over, steroid body, enormous, gigantic, physically intimidating man, wearing a red Strand t-shirt. So I let him in, seemed very nice, he pulled out a laptop, turned it on, said, "I'm just going to take a look at the books, if you wouldn't mind." "Fine, no problem." I left him alone, went upstairs, about ten minutes later, he calls up to me. Which should have been the first red flag – it only took him ten minutes – and he said, "I have a price." "Oh. OK, how much?" He said, "Two thousand dollars." I said, "Wow. Two thousand dollars? For two thousand books?" They're gonna end up on those dollar bookcarts on 12th Street. He said, "We have to make a profit." "I know, but—" I remember pointing to that series, to "The Drama," I said, "I've seen that listed online, the complete set, for a thousand dollars. A thousand dollars. For those twenty books." And he said, "Just because it's listed for a thousand dollars, doesn't mean it's worth a thousand dollars. In fact, if it's listed for a thousand dollars and it hasn't sold? By definition, it's worth less than a thousand dollars." Well, he's got me there. With logic. "But they have to be worth several hundred, a few hundred, at least. And 'America's Lost Plays,' twenty volumes, that's got to be worth several hundred, too. And there are a lot of other books that are worth twenty, forty, fifty dollars, easily." A dollar a book was just ridiculous, so I said, "I'm sorry, but I'm not gonna do it." And we shook hands, no hard feelings, and then he said, "Do you want to pay me in cash or with a check?" "For what?" "For the assessor's fee." I said, "I know nothing about an assessor's fee." He said, "There's always an assessor's fee. For any collection over fifteen hundred books. It's in the contract." "Contract? What contract? I didn't sign any contract? There was no contract." He said, "There's always a contract." There was no contract. So he pulled out his cellphone, called the Strand, and he put me on with the guy from the— oh, the big guy's name was Gary! I just remembered that: Gary. So the guy at the Strand, the guy I talked to a week ago, he reiterated everything Gary had said. There's always an assessor's fee for any collection over fifteen hundred books, it's in the contract, we don't send an assessor out unless there's a signed contract so you must have signed it, and if you didn't sign it it's your fault, so finally I was just fed up, I wanted this over with and I wanted this guy out of my house, so I said, "Fine. How much is the assessor's fee?" And he says, "Five hundred dollars." "That's ridiculous! Five hundred dollars? I'm not gonna do it. If I'd signed a contract, I'd pay it, but I didn't sign a contract, so I'm not gonna pay." I hung up, I turned to Gary, I said, "Look, there was no contract. I'm sorry, but I didn't sign anything, it's nothing personal, but I'm not gonna pay the assessor's fee." And then he – did I mention how big he was? He was huge! – he started to get belligerent and threatened, not so subtly, bodily harm. And I was … honestly, scared. And he got more and more exercised, and I remember, at one point he said, "Can you see my ass crack?" "Can I see your … what? No! I don't know what that means!" And he said, "Do I look like a plumber to you?" I think he meant, are my pants way down here, if I was a plumber, you could see my— and I said, "No. No, Gary. You don't look like a plumber and I can't see your ass crack. I don't know where you're going with this." And he said, "If I was a plumber, this would be an estimate. Which is free. But I'm not a plumber, and this is not an estimate. I am an assessor, and that's an art, assessing, and I deserve to be paid for that. For my art." He was furious, like popping-neck-veins furious. And I was alone in the house. And I was … I didn't want to get beaten up. I wish I could report that I was brave and I told him to fuck off and I called the cops, but I wasn't. And I didn't. I was scared. Though I was brave enough to talk him down. To three hundred and fifty dollars. Cash.

Groans from the audience.

I know. I know. Two weeks later, I was in the neighborhood, I went into the Strand, still kind of traumatized, just to lodge a formal complaint. I said, "I called you guys about a month ago, I have two thousand theater books, this man came out to my apartment, from your Assessors Department, big guy named Gary, the guy behind the counter said, very Strand-like, "We call it Appraisers." "OK. He said Assessors." "Well, we call it Appraisers." "Fine, but he called himself an assessor." "We say Appraisers." "Appraiser, assessor, whatever, it doesn't really matter, I just want to lodge a complaint." So I described him: Gary, six foot four, shaved head, goatee, tattoos, muscles. The guy said, "There's nobody who works here who fits that description. In fact, there's not even anyone named Gary. There was a Gary, like, three years ago, but he was short and skinny and he had really long hair." And then he said, with like a half-smile, "I think you've been conned." Yes. Yes, I have. I've been conned. "And I think it was an inside job. If you called and talked to somebody here, he's probably got something going on on the side, they're looking for rubes like you who would pay five hundred dollars. That's probably what happened." "But when I called back, I talked to somebody at the— oh, shit." "Yeah, he made that phone call, right? On his cellphone?" "Well, is there any way to, ya know, try to figure out who it was? I mean, it's one of your employees." And he said there wasn't, it could have been anybody, there was a really quick turnover, and there was really nothing he could do about it. And then he said – I'll never forget this – he said, with that same half-smile, "A perfect hoax is a work of art." I thought, Are you fucking kidding me? I just got conned for three hundred and fifty dollars and you're giving me a fucking aphorism? And then he said, very smug, "That's Dostoyevsky!" And I thought, Jesus Christ, that's the Strand in a nutshell. I'm smarter than you, I'm better read than you, and I'm going to quote Dostoyevsky at you. I was livid. About the whole thing. Because, though there was no written contract, there was a social contract between Gary and me. He said he was something, and I believed him, and he tricked me. And it took me a month or so to get over it, to figure it out, and here's the place I am now – and I know this is self-delusional, so please don't disabuse me of this self-protective certainty: I think it was three hundred and fifty dollars well spent. Because I spent that much money to discover that I didn't want to sell the books. To the Strand or to anyone else. And that led me to try to give them away to Exeter, which turned into a disaster. Which led me, finally, to this. I see some people nodding. I've convinced you! Good, because I've almost convinced myself. I was taken. There was this hoax, this trick, but it led me to a better place, a deeper truth. Anyway, that's my story, and I'm sticking to it. For now, at least. Needless to say, I rarely go into the Strand these days. I just … I guess I don't have any desire to relive that memory.

Hands the book to AUDIENCE MEMBER 6.

There you go.

Records the author and title on the index card. Next book.

OK. Next book. "Simpatico," by Sam Shepard. Who chose this?

AUDIENCE MEMBER 7

I chose that.

ED SCHMIDT

And why "Simpatico"?

AUDIENCE MEMBER 7

Well, I'm a big fan of Sam Shepard, and I've never read this one. I took a class at the New School, in probably 1992, David Mamet and Sam Shepard and—

ED SCHMIDT

Not them, their plays.

AUDIENCE MEMBER 7

Right, their plays. Wouldn't it be great if it was them?

ED SCHMIDT

Yes! Yes, it would! Well, Mamet I'm not so sure about. I love his plays, I'm just not sure I'd want to be lectured at by David Mamet for a whole semester.

AUDIENCE MEMBER 5

Sam Shepard's not a very nice person.

ED SCHMIDT

Oh, is that right?

AUDIENCE MEMBER 5

Yeah.

ED SCHMIDT

I hadn't heard that! Can I spread that rumor?

AUDIENCE MEMBER 5

Please. He's a real asshole. I mean …

ED SCHMIDT

He's easy on the eyes, though, isn't he?

AUDIENCE MEMBER 5

I guess. If you like that sort of …

ED SCHMIDT

We'll agree to disagree.

AUDIENCE MEMBER 5

On his looks. Not his personality.

ED SCHMIDT

Fair enough. His plays, his early plays, I mean, we can all agree – well, maybe not all of us, but most people can agree – that the early plays – some of those one acts, then "True West," "Fool for Love," "Buried Child" – those are extraordinary plays. In the American canon, no question. His later ones, I don't know, they've become less and less interesting. I'm not wild about "Simpatico." It's about horse racing. Are you familiar with it?

AUDIENCE MEMBER 7

No.

3 Plays

ED SCHMIDT

It was made into a movie. With, I think, Nick Nolte. Or Ed Harris. One of those. So. It's lesser Shepard, but it's Shepard. Who happens to be an asshole.

He stamps and dates the book. Hands it back.

There you go.

Records the author and title on the index card. Next book.

Edward Albee. "Three Tall Women."

AUDIENCE MEMBER 8

I picked that.

ED SCHMIDT

Why "Three Tall Women"?

AUDIENCE MEMBER 8

I like the playwright. I find him pretty daring. And I don't know this play at all. I'm familiar with the title, but I've not picked it up.

ED SCHMIDT

It's ... it's ... it's good. It's very good. Three actresses all playing the same character, at different stages in her life. Of his plays in the last ... fifteen years? ... I like "Three Tall Women" the most. And "The Goat." "The Goat" is brilliant. You're right, he's a restless, daring playwright, and this one, he's always experimenting with form and style, and you can see, with a play like this, that he's, at heart, a product of that Off Off Broadway revolution in the '60s. I hope you read it, you'll like it.

Pause.

God, I can't believe I actually suggested you read a play! Well. They're valueless only

93

to me. You'll like it.

As he stamps and dates the book.

I took a playwriting course with Albee once.

AUDIENCE MEMBER 8

Really?

ED SCHMIDT

Yeah. Long time ago. It was a one-day master class.

Hands the book back.

AUDIENCE MEMBER 8

Thank you.

ED SCHMIDT

You're welcome.

As he records the author and title on the index card.

The artistic director of the theater company I was working for in the mid-eighties, she knew Albee, and she brought him in for this class. There were five or six of us and he was extraordinary. Bright and funny and charismatic and … he was a little prickly – not sure he really wanted to be there – but he was, as you can imagine, inspiring, but he had this theory about playwriting that I thought was incredibly simple, or simplistic, and, I thought, reductive. Basically, his theory was this: All playwriting is about manipulation. About trickery and subterfuge and lying. The better a liar you are, the better a manipulator you are, the better a playwright you are. And he set up this very sort of antagonistic relationship between the playwright and the audience, which I loathed. Because it struck me as ungenerous. And the interesting thing is, his plays don't reflect that. They're not manipulative, not in that way. Some of them are more conventional and they manipulate the audience in the ways of standard narrative structure, but they're not cynical. I think he's one of those people who – and I know he taught, at the university level, in Texas, I think – and maybe it's the kind of thing where he's a great practitioner, but not a very good teacher. He doesn't practice what he preaches. There was a line from Shaw that he quoted – I'm paraphrasing, because it was many years ago – um … "The playwright's only task is to convince the audience that real things are happening to real people." Which, I think, is one task in one kind of play, but when he talked about manipulating the audience, I thought, If I ever become a playwright, I vow not to write those kinds of plays, that set up an intentionally antagonistic relationship where you're trying to pull one over on the audience. I vowed not to do that.

Pause.

And look where that's gotten me.

Next book.

Let's see … "Bells Are Ringing."

AUDIENCE MEMBER 9

That's me.

ED SCHMIDT

That's yours. Comden and Green. Why "Bells Are Ringing"?

AUDIENCE MEMBER 9

There was a production at Encores a few months back. And the script had been rewritten, by David Ives. So I wanted to look at the original script.

ED SCHMIDT

The real thing.

Ed Schmidt

AUDIENCE MEMBER 9

Yes.

ED SCHMIDT

I remember seeing Adolph Green on the street once. Just outside the Plaza Hotel. He had an enormous head. Only Soupy Sales had a larger head. True story. Not very relevant, but true.

Pages through the book, stops.

Oh. Oh. Did you see the bookplate here?

Shows it to the audience.

The City of Asheville Public Library. Stamped withdrawn. So I didn't steal this one.

Looks at the bookplate for several seconds. The rest of this speech does not come easily.

Wow. I remember where I … huh. Sorry. Wow. Just a flood. Um. Totally forgotten. Wow. I remember where I … who gave this to me, and where I was when I got it. Um. My father. Taught at the Asheville School, in Asheville, North Carolina. From age sixty-five to seventy-five. And … um … he worked at many boarding schools … throughout the years … and … this was … his last. So this had to be … 2000 … 4? 5? I used to go up to the Adirondacks, to stay with my parents, every summer, two or three weeks, and I'd always bring a stack of plays to read. And my father, who really knew nothing about the theater, but he was supportive, of course, and occasionally he'd see something like this, at a used book store or a library sale, and he … I remember it was … wow … my mother was … it all comes back … it was evening, my mother was cooking us dinner and my father was returning from a trip to … New Hampshire! … right, a school he used to teach at there, the Tilton School, was dedicating a … room? I think. In the History library – yeah, it was a study room, with a plaque, honoring his years of service to the school, and he came back home, and my sister was there, and my father came back from the trip and we had dinner, and then I went out on the porch. They'd cut down dozens and dozens of trees, so we had a clear view of the Adirondack range – Giant and Algonquin and Big Slide – and he went back in, I was reading something, and he went back into his study and he came back out with a couple of books that he'd brought from Asheville, for me, and this was one of them. And it was just the two of us, out on the porch, and, uh, yeah. I started reading this. And he was reading the New York *Times*.

Pause. Just remembers.

And he made us Manhattans. Which was his drink of choice. With a teaspoon of maple syrup. His secret ingredient. Talk about insignificant details. Yeah. I don't think I would have remembered that moment … unless I'd opened up this book and seen this bookplate. Wow. It's funny how these books, these objects, can be mnemonic devices. Um. OK.

Stamps and dates and hands it back. Records the author and title on the index card. Next book, last book.

Last book. "The Modern Stage in Latin America: Six Plays."

AUDIENCE MEMBER 10

Me.

ED SCHMIDT

That's you.

AUDIENCE MEMBER 10

Yeah. My family's Brazilian. And I've never really seen a play in Brazil, and my Portuguese is ok, it isn't amazing, and I probably wouldn't read this in Portuguese, and the other plays looked interesting, too. I love how plays, like, really reflect what's going on in a culture and a country, and through that lens, plus, it would be, like, very difficult to find that book if I were, like, in a bookstore.

ED SCHMIDT

I agree.

AUDIENCE MEMBER 10

And I was looking at Molière and maybe wanting to read the play you mentioned, "The …" what was it called?

ED SCHMIDT

"Le Malade Imaginaire." "The Imaginary Invalid."

AUDIENCE MEMBER 10

Yeah, but, I was, like, I could probably find that.

ED SCHMIDT

Yes, you could. This is much harder to find. No, I sympathize, or empathize, I'm not sure what the right one is. Before I traveled to Italy, I read Goldoni, and before I went to France, I read Molière. When I traveled to Czechoslovakia, I read Václav Havel. This romantic notion of trying to understand a culture by reading its plays, it's very seductive. I don't know. I don't think it works, frankly. It's as good an idea as any, though, I suppose. I guess you can learn about America by reading "Speed-the-Plow." You probably can.

AUDIENCE MEMBER 10

It'll probably sit on my shelf.

ED SCHMIDT

That's OK.

3 Plays

AUDIENCE MEMBER 10

I'll probably never read it.

ED SCHMIDT

That's OK. It's red, it'll jump out. People'll say, "'The Modern Stage in Latin America'? You must be very smart!"

AUDIENCE MEMBER 10

But there's a good story behind it.

ED SCHMIDT

What's the story?

AUDIENCE MEMBER 10

That I got it at your play.

ED SCHMIDT

Oh, yes! "What's the story?" Jesus. OK. Yes. I'm a little slow. There is a good story behind it.

As he stamps and dates the book, records the author and title on the index card. Everything from here to the end of the play is scripted.

So, this is it. The end. Or very nearly. The last play. My last play. For tonight, at least.

Counts the audience.

Ten. Ten more books gone. Ten more inanimate objects, mnemonic devices, off my shelves and out the door. Ten more gaps in the shelves. Ten more twenty-dollar bills in my pocket. Ten more empty chairs. Ten steps closer to the end. And I want to thank you for your role in that. I'm going to read the last lines of my last play, and then the lights will fade and you will applaud – I hope – the lights will rise, I will bow – the old time-honored traditions of the theater. I might even do that European kind of thing, where I applaud you. As if we're all in this together. Even though we're not. But who knows? Sentiment might get the better of me in that moment. And then I will exit through what would be, if this were a proper play, curtains, and spend a diva-like five minutes upstairs, decompressing, and then come back down, and if anyone would like to stick around and chat, that would be fine, and if no one would, that'd be fine, too. I would love to go out with you afterwards, all of you, for a drink or something, or to eat – I'm starving, I haven't had anything since breakfast – but I can't. I'm sure that disappoints you, but I can't. As much as I would like to, I can't. I have to walk away. Actually, you have to walk away; I have to stay here, with my books, until they're all gone, and then maybe, perhaps, hopefully, after they're all gone, I will be able to join you. If you do plan to go out – that would be nice. That just occurred to me – all ten of you, going out together, for dinner and drinks, the communal nature of the theater. There are a couple of nice restaurants in the neighborhood. If you hit Court Street and turn right, there's Buttermilk Channel and Frankie's and Prime Meats, which are probably all packed. There's a little Spanish tapas place in that area. If you turn left on Court, there's a Thai … you know what, now I'm starting to manipulate you. I vowed I would not write those kinds of plays. So, do whatever the hell you want when you leave. I want no control.

Pause.

Speaking of which. I have a quick confession to make. Two minutes. Before it's too late. I don't know how to say this except directly.

Pause.

Those were not Molière's last words. I don't know what they were, but "Crève! Crève!" "Choke! Die!" was not … he did, in fact, cough up blood into a handkerchief late in the third act of the fourth public performance of "Le Malade Imaginaire," but he made it through to the end, and he collapsed backstage. The show must go on. And he was transported back to his home, where he faded in and out of consciousness for the next several hours, and he died the next day. So, I don't know what his last words were, but they were not "Crève! Crève!" And I know, that was the bookseller's story, but it's not real. The handkerchief is real, but the story is not.

A beat.

And Shakespeare did not write "The Tempest" at forty-eight. He wrote it at forty-seven. But when I discovered that fact, I was forty-seven, and it made so much sense, and then time, as time is wont to do, moved on, and I became forty-eight, and Shakespeare remained forty-seven, and it was such a good story that the only way to get it in there was to change his age or my age, and I decided to change his age instead. So. He was forty-seven when he wrote "The Tempest."

A beat.

And Shakespeare didn't coin the phrase "For all intents and purposes." Why I said that, I have no idea. And I didn't run track in high school and I never met Peter Brook and I didn't take a playwriting course with Edward Albee and I did not read all these plays. I read a lot of them, but I didn't read them all. That would be ridiculous. And I never worked at the Strand and the story about my ... but I am ... I am an artist, and this is what separates us from the other ... I mean, we create these narratives that might not necessarily be true, but somehow we ... no, that's ... bullshit.

To AUDIENCE MEMBER 1.

I hope to God you really are an acting teacher.

Or whatever factual tidbit had been offered earlier by an AUDIENCE MEMBER.

AUDIENCE MEMBER 1

I am.

ED SCHMIDT

That may be the only real thing about tonight. Except the books! The books are real. The books are real. The books are real, and they are going out the door, and that is real. I mean, the events of this evening will go, and the name of the girl you kissed in high school will go, and your memories will go, and you will go, and Adolph Green is gone, but his book is still here. The books are real. Par la mort non de diable, as the devil is my witness, the books are real, and my father is gone and I hope – I trust – that that is enough.

He opens to the last page of "The Modern Stage in Latin America."

The last lines of my last play.

He pretends to read the last lines of the last play, but actually he recites the last lines of "Our Town."

"There are the stars doing their old, old crisscross journeys in the sky. Scholars haven't settled the matter yet, but they seem to think there are no living beings up there. Just chalk. Or fire. Only this one is straining away, straining away all the time just to make something of itself. The strain's so bad that every sixteen hours everybody lies down and gets a rest."

He closes the book, hands it to AUDIENCE MEMBER 10. *Looks at his watch.*

"8:57 [or whatever time it actually is] in Grover's Corners. You get a good rest, too. Good night."

The lights fall.

The End

OUR LAST GAME

Cast & Production

Our Last Game opened on August 25, 2015, in a locker room at the Nord Anglia International School, on 44 East 2nd Street, New York City. It closed on November 1, 2015.

Ed Schmidt played the role of COACH.

3 Plays

PREGAME

(2003)

Before entering the locker room, an usher gives one audience member a clipboard and a one-page scouting report. He or she will be COACH K. Every other audience member receives a "SPARTANS" warmup jacket to wear.

The locker room door opens and the audience files in. A few benches. Barely enough room for fifteen. A metal folding chair. On one wall, a large dry-erase basketball board. A clock reads 6:20.

After a few minutes, COACH enters. He is 62 years old. He wears pleated khakis, a slightly-too-roomy button-down shirt, a Spartans necktie. No jacket. Comfortable, thick-soled, black dress shoes. Eyeglasses on his head. He carries a scorebook and a pencil.

He is tired. He walks with a slight limp: his right knee has never been the same since surgery, and he'll need a hip replacement in a year or two.

He unfolds the metal chair, sits, opens the scorebook, puts on his glasses, begins filling out the starting lineup.

COACH

After a minute or so, almost to himself, without looking up.

How much time do we have?

No answer. He looks at COACH K.

Coach K? Time is it?

COACH K

Looking at his watch.

8:10.

COACH

8:10!?

He looks at the wall clock. It reads 6:22.

It's 6:22.

Gimme a heart attack. Your watch is fast.

Or, if COACH K says "6:22," the previous lines are cut.

Plenty of time.

He continues filling out the starting lineup. After several seconds, pauses, stumped.

The hell am I missing?

He looks around the room. Mumbles each player's name, can't figure out who he's missing. Finally, it dawns on him.

Michael Kearley. You're like a ghost over there.

He records Michael Kearley's name and number, closes the scorebook. He stands.

OK. Starting lineup ... Peter, Arthur, Eddie, John McN—

Realizes something.

No. That's not right. It is ... Senior Night.

Returns to the scorebook, starts erasing and adding.

3 Plays

So. Starting five are the five Seniors. Joe D. Eddie. J.O. John McNicholas. John McCarthy.

They're going to do the whole Senior Night thing, so. Very quick. Let's not drag it out. We actually have a game to play. After warmups, I'll say a few words. Midcourt, short and sweet, about the Seniors. Then I'll call you up. Rest of the team stay on the bench, with Coach K. I'll call each of the Seniors up, one at a time. Seniors, do me a favor: jog. Don't walk, don't look like you're bored or embarrassed; this is not for you, it's for your parents, so – jog to me, firm handshake, Mom and Dad, hug and a kiss, flowers, photo … I think there's a photo, too. Right? Coach K, is there a photo?

>COACH K *doesn't know.*

How the hell did we do it in the past? Check on that.

>COACH K *will check on that.*

Ask Ms. Stillman, she'll know.

Ya know what, forget about the photo. Tell her that: no photo.

And five minutes, no more.

Everybody got it? Yes? Questions.

>*No questions.*

Coach K. Scouting report.

COACH K

>*Reading from the scouting report on his clipboard.*

Ithaca. 20 wins, 2 losses. Currently #2 in the state.

Offense averages 82 points. Defense: 56.

Ed Schmidt

COACH

They run. Run and run and run. These guys love to run.

Gonna have to work hard to hold em to 48.

12 a quarter. That's our goal: 12 a quarter.

Motions to COACH K *to continue.*

COACH K

Reading the scouting report.

Defense: Diamond and 1 press after every made basket. Usually into a man-to-man, sometimes into a 1-3-1.

COACH

That's after a make. We went through this.

Nods for COACH K *to continue.*

COACH K

After a miss, they drop back—

COACH

Against the press …

Going to the whiteboard. Can't find his marker.

Where the hell is my …

Patting his pockets, looking around.

Coach, do you have my … ah!

3 Plays

He spots the marker Velcroed to the board. Demonstrates.

Against the press. Diamond and one. Simple.

Diamond and ... one.

Ball, two at the foul line, two at half court.

Pass comes in, they trap. Everybody see this? Get where you can see it.

They trap, immediately look where?

> *Looks around, no answer. Waits.*

Middle.

Yes? Blank stares, Coach.

Look middle.

Then wing.

That's not open, he slides over, denies ... inbounder – that's you tonight, J.O., step in, you're the release.

Bounce pass, he breaks sideline, flashes middle, swing it, get the ball in the middle.

And no dribbles. No dribbles. We don't dribble against the diamond and one. Ball doesn't touch the floor until we hit the middle.

And then what?

> *No response.*

Then what?

> *No response.*

The drill at the beginning of practice.

No response. He's starting to get frustrated.

Attack. Yes? Get the ball in the middle and attack. Score. Make em pay.

They throw this press at us, you're not ready, three, four turnovers, we're down ten in a heartbeat. Game's over. Exactly what happened at their gym.

You're not ready, we're gonna get slaughtered.

I would prefer not to get slaughtered in our last game.

Long pause. To COACH K.

Continue, Coach.

COACH K

Reading the scouting report.

After a miss, they drop back into a man-to-man.

Run the offenses. Run the box, run the weave, run motion.

Run each offense all the way through.

COACH

All the way through. Run the offense all the way through.

Run it, run it, run it, run it.

I know some of you boys don't believe in the offense. I know. Most of your parents don't believe in the offense. They've made that clear.

Half the people in the gym don't believe in it.

3 Plays

Pointing to COACH K.

This guy averaged 36 points a game. Before the 3-pointer. Running the box, the weave, and motion.

The offense worked in 1984, it still works. If you run it.

"But, Coach, the other team knows our offense better than we do!"

They probably do. God bless em.

So, we will not get the basket cut off the first pass. Maybe not even the fourth or the fifth. But on the sixth pass, the seventh, maybe even the eighth, when they know what's coming, they jump the cut, that's when we go backdoor, that's when we get a layup.

So, run it, run it, run it.

Trust me on this, boys. You have not, some of you, all year. You have fought me, and I've fought you, and what's been the result? 8 and 14.

I've been doing this for a long time. I know a little something about the game of basketball.

Run the offense, run it patiently, run it through, run it over and over and over.

We will score against this team.

They're good. 20 and 2, like coach said.

You hear the other coaches in the league, they're starting to talk, this might be a great team. One for the ages.

They're not.

Thirty-three years in this league I've seen three great teams.

Troy, four years ago. They were great.

Athens, my second year – lost their first game, won twenty-six in a row. State champs.

And us in '84. Undefeated. Undefeated going into the tournament, we played one bad first half of basketball, that's it. In the semi-finals of the state tournament. Because we weren't ready.

Down twenty-two, stormed back, lost by a point. Down twenty-two, at halftime, we almost won.

Ran out of— we didn't lose, we ran out of time. That game had been a minute longer, we'd a been State champs.

Lost to a team we'd beat twice already. By double figures. The next night, they went out and won States. By …

> *Looks to* COACH K *for confirmation.*

… sixteen, seventeen? That was our trophy. Ask Coach K.

So, I've seen great teams, I've coached a great team.

This team, tonight? They're not a great team. They're good. Better than us. And 32's a helluva ballplayer. Best this league has seen since Coach.

But they could not have beaten our '84 team. Not a chance. With Coach? Reggie DeGroff? Wally Huchro? Lydamore? Tyler? The Vanderhoof brothers?

My son? Thomas? He could shoot.

> *Pause.*

Couldn't beat em.

This team we can beat. Not the '84 team. Ithaca.

If. We control the tempo. Slow the game. Use the clock. The clock is our friend. Take time off the clock.

3 Plays

Run the offense over and over and over. No quick shots. Keep the clock running.

Same thing on defense. No quick shots. Pressure on the ball. Make them take time off the clock. Every possession. As they see those minutes tick down, they will start to panic. And then they'll make mistakes.

All right. Quick review.

> *At the whiteboard again.*

They run this 5 out. 32's on the wing. They run pick away for him. Back pick, down pick, they'll set a cross pick. Pick away, constantly.

So we must have ball pressure.

Pressure on the ball we force where?

> *No answer.*

J.O., your big start tonight. Pressure on the ball, we force where?

> *J.O. doesn't know.*

You don't know.

Peter, please remind J.O., pressure on the ball, we force where?

> PETER *doesn't answer. Losing his patience.*

Weak hand. Yes? Weak hand. On the ball, we force our man to his weak hand. He's right-handed, we force him where? Left. Weak hand.

Pressure on the ball, we force weak hand.

Coach and I have been preaching this all season. Entire season. Day one. Pressure on the ball, we force weak hand.

> *Back to the whiteboard.*

OK. One pass away, in the gap, in help. He drives, step in, anticipate help, help and recover. Two passes away, one foot in the lane, full help.

Ball swings, everybody moves. Pressure on the ball, we force where?

SOMEONE

Weak hand.

COACH

Weak hand. One pass away, in the gap. Two passes away, one foot in the lane.

Ball picks. They don't set many, but we switch on all ball picks.

Pick away, we go where?

No answer.

Pick away, we go where?

No answer. Nearly at the breaking point.

Come on, we reviewed this in practice yesterday!

Pick away, we go under. Does this ring a bell? Pick away, we go under. Step back, hand on the hip, usher him through, go under.

These are our defensive principles, boys. Coach and I have preached this since November 1st. Every day. Four months.

If you don't know this, we have wasted four months.

Do you not remember? Have you forgotten?

Or is it me? Is it my fault? Maybe it's my fault. Me and Coach K. Our fault. Did we not say it often enough? Or loud enough? Did we not preach our defensive principles, what we believe in, did we not preach what we believe in often enough or loud enough or convincingly enough? Or entertainingly enough?

Did we not entertain you? Did we bore you? In practice. For four months. Maybe that's what happened. You were bored. We bored you. We bored them, Coach K.

Or do you not care? You don't care. You heard us, you listened to us, you understood us, what we wanted, what we believe in, you just decided to do something else.

    Long pause.

Or maybe you just forgot. Teenagers, that's your job.

Maybe you just forgot.

    Pause. He's angry, frustrated, exhausted.

I know you're tired. Been a long, frustrating season. Half of you can't wait for baseball to start. For this to end.

Me, too. Me, too, boys. I'm exhausted, too.

    Pause.

Last game. Meaningless. 8 and 14. One more meaningless game. And then it's over.

But, god … then it's over. This is it. Tonight. This is our last game.

The last time we will be together, as a group. As a team. If that means anything to you.

Seniors, tonight is the last time you'll wear the Spartans uniform.

I know, baseball season. But then what? Then what?

This ends. It ends.

Maybe you're too young. To get it.

Maybe, Coach K, they're too young to get it.

But you will.

Someday.

> *Pause. He looks at the clock.*

That right?

OK. Let's go. Warmups. Everybody up.

> *Hesitation.*

Up.

> *Everyone starts to stand. But not with the enthusiasm he would like. He stares at them for several seconds.*

Ya know what? We have time. Sit.

> *Exploding with rage.*

SIT!!!!!

Sit.

> *Everyone sits. Pause.*

This is our last game, and that's your sense of urgency? That's all the passion you can muster?

We're not going to States. We can't win the league. We can't even go 500. This game, tonight, our last game, in the standings, means nothing. Changes nothing. Doesn't matter if we win or lose. 8 and 15 or 9 and 14.

Either way, we wake up tomorrow morning, we were a losing team.

If that's what you want people to remember – a losing team – I'm sixty-two years old, I got a fake knee and a hip that's shot to hell, I'll sit. I could use the rest. I won't get out of my chair tonight.

Roll the ball out, run your own offense. To hell with ya.

Get beat by 35, that's what you want.

Or. You can fight like hell.

And maybe – probably not, but maybe – win.

People might remember that.

8 and 14. Last game of the season. Meaningless. Nothing to gain. Against Ithaca. 20 and 2. Powerhouse. Dominant program in the state. Ya know what? They fought like hell.

It's up to you. I can't make you do it. I don't understand you.

>*Pause.*

Captains, you have anything to say? Johnny Mac?

>*Nothing.*

No? J.O., anything?

>*Nothing.*

Nothing. OK.

>*Pause. Looks at the clock.*

We're late.

I'll ask the officials to put a few more minutes on the clock.

>*He looks around. Something hits him.*

Ed Schmidt

I wasn't going to say anything. Let you find out in a few weeks, when the official announcement came. But I think you boys should know.

This is my last game, too.

I'm not going to coach next year.

Teach through the spring, full pension, retire.

Only person I've told is Ms. Stillwell.

Mark, I apologize. I haven't even told Coach K.

And Doc Robinson knows. I have ... um. It's time. I have a health ... issue. So. While I have some time. Travel, visit my daughter, spend some time with the grandkids. It's time.

And with the new gym going up next year, this old rattrap coming down. It's about time.

I don't know what'll happen. The school has to go through the whole interview process, open the job up. It's state law. But I think Coach K would make a terrific head coach. He knows the system, the program, and he can continue what we've been doing.

And you've been a great assistant for ... five years now? Four?

And I told Ms. Stillwell. You boys feel the same way, let her know.

So. Whoever gets the job – Coach, if it's you; and you boys who are returning next year – I promise I won't put you in the same position I was in my first year. With Coach Raymond. The legendary Coach Raymond.

I won't show up to all your practices, all your games. In the locker room, on the bench. Which is what he did.

I won't stand over your shoulder, constantly tell you what you're doing wrong, and then badmouth you behind your back. Like he did.

I've said too much. We have time to talk about that.

In the spring.

> *He looks at the clock.*

Plenty of time.

> *Pause.*

Last game.

> *Pause.*

I just want to say.

> *Starts to choke up.*

I have loved every …

> *He weeps, long and hard. Finally recovers.*

OK. OK. OK.

We have a game to play. Everybody up.

> *Hesitation. Everyone stands.*

Hands in.

> *Hands in.*

One last time. On three, Spartans. One, two, three …

EVERYONE

Spartans!

Ed Schmidt

He looks at the team. They haven't moved.

COACH

Go! Coach K, lead em out. I'll be with you in a minute.

COACH K *leads the team out.*

And ask them to put some more time on the clock.

End of Pregame

3 Plays

HALFTIME

(1984)

The door opens and the players file in. The large dry-erase board has been replaced by a large blackboard. On the blackboard are a few messily drawn, barely decipherable plays and the words "NO REGRETS."

An older clock on the wall reads 7:55.

In this scene, the audience member who played COACK K *will play* MARK KEARLEY, *the 18-year-old version of* COACH K. *Another audience member will be the current assistant coach –* COACH EVERETT. *During the break, an usher has given* COACH EVERETT *a scorebook and quickly taught him or her how to read it.*

COACH *enters. He carries a chalkboard eraser and a clipboard that holds the first-half stat sheet. He wears slacks, a white dress shirt, a V-neck sweater-vest. And a wedding band. He does not wear glasses.*

Until COACH *"sits, spent," this should be a full-out tirade. Shocking in its intensity and volume.*

COACH

I'm lost! I am lost!

Can somebody please tell me what the hell is going on, because I am lost!

47 to 25! 47— what is our goal? 48! 12 a quarter! And we just gave up 47 in one half!

In the semi-finals of the fucking state tournament!

Throws the eraser.

To a team ... I don't give a shit who hears ... to a team we beat twice already. Cleared the fucking bench! And they're beating us by 22?

No! No!

They're gonna take away our chance at a state championship?

No!

We are better than them!

We shoot the ball better, we rebound better, we play better defense, and we are so much better coached than they are it's not even fucking funny!

And we're down 22?

With the best player in the state on our team? The best. 36 points a game.

Coach Everett, how many points does Mark Kearley have?

COACH EVERETT

Consulting the scorebook.

Four.

COACH

Four points. On ...

Consulting the stat sheet.

... five shots.

3 Plays

Calmly approaches MARK KEARLEY, *squats in front of him.*

Shoot the ball, Mark. Shoot it. Shoot it, shoot it, shoot it, shoot it, SHOOT THE FUCKING BALL!

Son, you are the best ballplayer I have ever coached. You are the best ballplayer I will ever coach. But tonight? In the biggest game of your— the biggest game of my life, you are shitting your pants.

You better turn it around. Because if you don't, you will regret this day for the rest of your life. I am not bullshitting you. You will never forget, because I won't let you forget, that you had one chance, and you fucked it up!

Live with that.

To THOMAS.

And Thomas, what the hell are you doing? What in God's name?

Everything I have ever taught you, every hour I have spent with you in the gym, in the driveway, at the hoop that I nailed to the side of the fucking garage!

Trying to teach you how to shoot a goddamn jump shot, day after day after day, hour after hour, with your mother screaming to put the ball away and come inside and get your homework done and go to bed, after all that, and you can't hit the broad side of a fucking barn in the one game that matters! All that time wasted!

Coach Everett, how many points does Thomas have?

A pause as COACH EVERETT *scans the scorebook.*

Don't tell me, because I know. Zero. Zero. That means nothing. You have given us nothing, you have contributed nothing, you have accomplished nothing!

You, son, are fucking killing us.

Consulting the stat sheet again.

Thirteen offensive rebounds. Thirteen! What is our goal? Six. Three a half. And we've given up thirteen.

You don't need to be a fucking math teacher to know that's disgraceful!

> *To* IKE TYLER.

Tyler, are you gonna get off your fat ass and get a defensive rebound? Are you?

> IKE *nods*.

Then do it! Shot goes up, turn around, sit into him, drive him back, and go get the ball! Every single time!

Or I'll sit you at the end of the bench and find somebody who will.

Hell, I'll put fucking Elbert in!

And they have gotten every loose ball! Every single one!

> *Demonstrating, bending over tentatively.*

Peter, this is you. Danny.

Grow a pair and dive on the floor!

"I'll dive on it next time, Coach." "I forgot the offense this time down the court, Coach, but I'll remember next time." "I'm not gonna make it to the state finals this year, Coach, but I'll get there next time!"

There is no next time! This is it! Now! This is the next time!

We are losing because they want it more than you! They want the ball, they want a trip to the state finals more than you do!

Because you don't care! You don't fucking care if we win or lose! Well, I got news for you, boys: I care! I care! I care if we win or lose!

3 Plays

If you don't have the balls and the heart to dive on a loose ball, I'll fucking dive on it! I'll jump off the bench and run across the court and I'll dive on it!

Because this is no longer a test of your basketball ability, this is a test of your character! And you are failing! Miserably! Every single one of you! And I'll be goddamned if you're gonna take me down with you.

47 points!

Our ball pressure is pathetic! Ellie, your man has beaten you every time! Every time! Left! He's left-handed! Pressure on the ball, force where? Weak hand!

Then do it!

You boys better get your heads out of your asses right now!

The stat sheet again.

Sixteen turnovers. Jesus Christ!

Against that press! It's a diamond and one! We can break it with our eyes closed! It's the simplest press in the— James Naismith knew how to break the diamond and one!

Get the ball in the middle! Get it in the middle! Swing the ball and get it in the middle!

And don't dribble! Don't dribble!

Reggie, you're dribbling right up the sideline, right into the teeth of the trap! Wally, you're trying to dribble through it! Why in God's name are you dribbling anywhere against this press?

It's a 5th grade YMCA press that doesn't work in the semi-finals of the state tournament – unless you dribble!

Don't dribble! Don't dribble! Do not fucking dribble against the fucking diamond and one!

Ed Schmidt

He throws a chair.

You think this opportunity comes along every year? You think a trip to the state finals comes around every year? I have been coaching thirteen years and this is the first time I've even sniffed it! This is a once-in-a-lifetime opportunity, boys, and you are walking around with your heads up your asses and your dicks in your hands!

Wake up! Wake up!

This is not a game! This is not a game! Let me say that one more time for any of you children who may have forgotten: This is not a game!

Our goal – our one goal – has been state champions. I told you, on November 1st, that I would settle for no less.

With the talent and the potential we have, anything short of a championship is a failure!

It's not our dream, it's not our hope, it isn't something that would be nice to have. It is our right! We deserve it! I deserve it! I deserve to hold up that trophy tomorrow night and put it next to the three others that fucking Coach Raymond one! I deserve it!

Because failure was not part of the game plan! To just be another team, another losing team, another mediocrity, somebody else's stepping stone on the way to the championship, a bit player in somebody else's success story, that is not who I am!

This ends! This ends! Do you not get it! This ends!

Well, it sure as hell better not end for me tonight.

> *He sits, spent. Thinks. For a minute, at least. He looks at the clock. He thinks some more. Quietly, almost to himself.*

OK.

OK.

3 Plays

He stands, retrieves the chair, the eraser that he threw. His tone is different. He sits in the chair. He's calm, controlled, confident.

OK. We're gonna abandon the game plan completely. We're coming out of the man-to-man, they're killing it. We're gonna play a zone. 1-3-1 half-court trap. I know you've never learned it, I've never taught it. You're gonna learn now. So lean in, pay attention.

Pulling out his clipboard. He takes the stat sheet off.

This is the first half. It's over.

He crumples the stat sheet, tosses it.

All that matters is the second half.

Demonstrating on the chalkboard clipboard.

Once they see what we're in, they're gonna go into a 2-1-2. They'll be as surprised to see us playing this defense as we are.

Mark, you're at the point. Above half court, play it perpendicular, this way, make yourself wide, force them to pass over you. Ellie, you're on the baseline. You follow the ball. The ball's here, you're here. It swings, you're here. You're gonna have to bust your ass, corner to corner, the whole second half. Can you do it?

ELLIE *can.*

Ike, you're in the middle. One job: don't let the ball into the middle. Hand in front, three-quarters, front him if you have to, don't let the ball get in the middle.

Wings. We'll start Wally and ...

Looks at THOMAS, *considers starting him.*

... Reggie.

They cross half court, wing comes up, Mark, trap. We trap here and here, and in the corners. Ellie follows the ball, Ike denies middle. Opposite wing – this is where we're vulnerable – the diagonal pass – so you have to get back. But anticipate this, and look to steal it.

Ball swings. Wing comes up. Mark, turn and trap. Ellie, bust your ass to the corner. Ike, spin and deny. Opposite wing, drop back, but if we trap right – hands up, they have to throw up and over the top. Steal it and take it to the bucket.

Got it? OK.

We have no time outs left – I used them all – so we have to stop the clock other ways. Five-second calls, ten-second calls. They stretch this defense out for twelve, fifteen seconds, and we don't get a shot or a turnover, we have to foul them. Put them on the line, stop the clock. We can't let them hold the ball for three or four minutes.

Stop the clock, stop the clock, stop the clock. At all costs, stop the clock.

Against the press, diamond and one … you know what to do. Get the ball in the middle, swing it, no dribbles. Get the ball to Mark and attack. Score. Make em pay. And Mark, go straight to the bucket, don't pull up, don't settle for the jumper. Take it right at him, get the foul. Stop the clock.

And knock those shots down. No missed free throws.

There's a reason we shoot fifty free throws every practice. There's a reason I keep track of how many you make and I don't let you screw around. There's a reason we only shoot after sprints. When you're tired, you're exhausted. There's a reason we busted your asses – all of us – for four months – touchdowns, wind sprints, stairs, gorilla drills – there's a reason, and the reason is when somebody outscores you by 22 in the first half, you gotta outscore em by 23 in the second. Bury em.

OK. When they come out of the press – because they will, we'll get the ball to Mark, he'll score four, five times in a row, they'll have to come out of it. They're gonna fall back into that box and one.

Starting to draw it on the clipboard.

Totally new look against that. The box, the weave, motion, it's not working. Ellie, you're at the point. One wing here, the other wing on the strong side block. Ike, you're on the weak side block. Mark, you're here. You're a decoy. Pass comes to the wing …

Looks at the clock.

Oh, shit. We don't have time. OK. We'll learn it as we go. We'll learn it during dead balls, during breaks. Adjust on the fly. We'll do it, we'll get it.

Everybody up.

Everybody up.

Boys. We are losing. Badly. But. We have not lost. There is still time. Not much, but enough. It's only halftime. We're not dead yet.

Every man longs for meaning and fulfillment and purpose. To do something important. Something memorable. Something that matters.

This matters.

This matters.

This is not our last game. Tonight is not our last game. We're gonna storm back and we're gonna win, and we're gonna win tomorrow and we're gonna raise the trophy. We're gonna be state champs. We're gonna go down in history. A team for the ages. They'll tell stories about us. We will be heroes.

Hands in!

Hands in.

Like your lives depended on it. On three, Spartans! One, two, three …

EVERYBODY

Spartans!

COACH

Go!

The team exits.

End of Halftime

3 Plays

POSTGAME

(1971)

The team files in to the locker room. COACH *awaits them, standing on a bench. No clock, no boards on the walls. Just benches and white walls. He wears dark slacks, a black tie, a wool suit jacket. Wedding ring, no glasses. He holds a basketball. During the break, an usher has given an audience member a small black basketball chalkboard. He or she will be* COACH RAYMOND.

THOMAS *is now* TOMMY, *five years old.*

COACH *cheers the team on as they enter. This is a celebratory scene. The lines should hew closely to the script, but there's no need, in the post-victory excitement, for* COACH *to be word-perfect.*

COACH

That's a great win! What a win! What a win! Great win! It's about time! Hot baby! That's it, boys, great win! That's the way to end it! Good win! Good win!

MICHAEL LINDE *enters, last or nearly last.*

There he is! Michael Linde! What a shot!

He hops down, throws an arm around MICHAEL LINDE'*s shoulder.*

Game ball for Michael Linde!

He gives MICHAEL LINDE *the game ball. Everyone cheers.*

All right, I have one question for you. And I want you to be honest. With all your teammates, and with Coach Raymond.

That shot. That game-winning shot. That game-winning shot that you were not supposed to take. That was designed for Jamie to take. But you made it, so it's all right!

Tell us the truth. When you took that shot … were your eyes closed?

Slight pause.

They were! Coach Raymond and I saw! We had a perfect view, didn't we, Coach?

Who threw the pass? Robert! You couldn't see it, could you?

Tommy, I bet you couldn't see it from your end of the bench, could you?

Coach and I had the perfect … show us how you did it! Show us!

MICHAEL LINDE *hesitates.* COACH *takes the ball from him.*

You have no idea what you did! Because your eyes were closed!

Demonstrating.

He caught the ball, like this, the basket's behind him, Robert throws it in, he catches and he turns, and Coach and I could see him, one dribble, he takes one dribble, and he – I swear to God …

He imitates a ridiculous shot.

… he closed his eyes, kicks his leg up, over his shoulder, off the backboard and in!

Game-winning shot! Game ball, Michael Linde!

He hands the ball back to MICHAEL LINDE, *leads the applause.*

Tommy, have you ever seen that shot before?

    TOMMY *hasn't.*

No! And I'll tell you why you haven't. Because we've been practicing that shot in secret! Every Saturday morning, when you go to your biddy-league practice, the big guys on the Varsity have been secretly practicing the Michael Linde Shot! So we could unveil it for you in the last game!

It was skill, pure skill! And practice!

We're going home tonight, you and me, and we're gonna go out into the driveway, and you're gonna take two hundred Michael Linde Shots. And tomorrow morning, we're gonna wake up and you're gonna shoot two hundred more! And we're gonna practice every day, two hundred Michael Linde Shots, all spring and all summer, and when we come back November 1st, you're gonna be a better Michael Linde Shooter than Michael Linde himself!

    To COACH RAYMOND.

That's good coaching, that was that is!

Coach Raymond, if you had taught your boys the Michael Linde Shot – instead of the two-handed set shot, and the hook shot – you would've won five state championships! Ten!

They might've named the gym after you, but they're gonna put up a statue of Michael Linde out front that'll outlive us all!

    Imitates the Michael Linde Shot again.

Oh, my goodness! What a shot! I'm exhausted! Thank goodness that was our last game, because I don't know if I can take any more of that! You boys will be the death of me!

    He sits on the floor.

All right. Gimme five minutes.

Tommy, come here, sit next to your old man.

>TOMMY *sits next to his father.*

Gimme five minutes, then you can shower up, go see your parents, your friends – Michael, there is a line of cheerleaders, twelve deep, all waiting for your autograph. All I can say is, you will not lack for company tonight, young man.

Go out tonight and celebrate. Celebrate! You deserve this. What a season! Winning season! 10 and 9! You should be proud of yourselves.

This has been a long season – four months – we've worked hard for four months.

So celebrate. You deserve it. Go celebrate. At the Old Schoolhouse.

You didn't think I knew about the Old Schoolhouse, did you? I was a Senior at this place not so long ago, I spent a few nights at the Old Schoolhouse myself. I know what goes on at the Old Schoolhouse.

Celebrate. As a team. This is why we do this, for moments like this. In moderation, of course.

I'm gonna celebrate. My wife and I are going to celebrate, and – between you and me – probably not in moderation. So we're gonna need a babysitter. Anybody want to babysit Tommy and his little sister? Tommy, I know how much you'd like Michael to babysit you tonight, but he's gonna be a very busy young man out at the Old Schoolhouse tonight. Maybe we'll ask Grandma.

>*Standing.*

All right. First things first. I want to thank Coach Raymond. Big hand for Coach Raymond.

>*He leads the applause for* COACH RAYMOND.

Coach, I want to thank you for the guidance and the wisdom you have given me this year. The time you've put in – at every practice, every game – you have made me a better coach and us a better team.

You're a legend. There's no denying that. Three state titles and how many league championships?

Slight pause.

Don't pretend like you don't know, because you reminded me every day this season! Sixteen! "I won sixteen league championships."

And they named the gym after you! If I have a fraction of that success – give me one state title and a couple of— and name the drinking fountains after me! That I would consider a success.

And I hope and trust that you know the program is in good hands. That you've handed the baton to someone who's headed in the right direction. And I hope you and Carol can take a well-deserved rest, visit your kids, your grandkids, and spend some time in a place where it doesn't snow nine months out of the year!

Thank you.

He shakes COACH RAYMOND's *hand.*

This has not been an easy transition for Coach. Change is never easy. You boys will learn that as you get older. This is a man who's been doing something he loves for decades and decades, and has had great success doing it, and now he has to give it up. That's not easy for any man. And this transition hasn't been easy for me. I've had to walk into that gym, with his name on it, and his championship banners and his trophies, those are big shoes to fill. And it hasn't been easy for you – and not just because of the three Seniors who quit, because they didn't believe in what we're doing. But because I brought in a whole new system, and you bought into it, all of you, and I appreciate your patience and your trust.

I know how much Coach loves his zone defense, and the success he's had with it, but I firmly believe that the future of the sport is in the man-to-man defense. The personal responsibility of the man-to-man defense.

Now, I may be wrong. But it's my job to do what I believe is right.

Look at Tommy. Tommy loves his Sugar Frosted Flakes. Tell em how much you love your Sugar Frosted Flakes.

TOMMY

A lot.

COACH

A lot! He loves them a lot! Couple weeks ago, I was at the market, and I saw a box of Wheaties. And I thought, it's time this young man starts eating Wheaties, if he wants to grow up to be a big boy like you. So I bought them, brought them home, the next morning Tommy wakes up, he's greeted by a bowl of Wheaties.

I'm gonna tell em what you did.

He looks at the bowl, he looks at me, he picks up the bowl – it's got the spoon and the milk still in it – he holds it up over the carpet, looks me dead in the eye, and he turns the bowl over, drops it on the carpet. Turns around, not a word, and he walks out. Five years old, stubborn like his old man!

Now, I may be wrong, Sugar Frosted Flakes may be the healthiest cereal in the world, but I don't believe so. And it's my job as his father to do what I think is best for him.

And it's my job as your coach to do what I believe is best for you, for the program. And I think we're headed in the right direction. And the results bear that out. A winning season! 10 and 9. That's the first winning season we've had around here in a little while.

And next year, we're gonna be even better. Everybody's back. No Seniors. We're gonna win the league next year. We're gonna win the league, and we're gonna get into the tournament. And once you're in the tournament, anything can happen. Michael Linde can close his eyes and toss one up over his shoulder at the horn and it can bank in.

Within a few years, we're gonna be the best team in the league, the best team in central New York. We're gonna, before I leave this place, we're gonna be the dominant program, Class D, New York State. We will be the basketball program that other high schools look up to.

Because you work hard, you play with passion, and you believe in what you're doing.

When I was walking over to the gym tonight, up the hill – the Raymond Gymnasium! – I thought back to last spring, last summer – you remember? – when they were building this gymnasium. All those men – bricklayers, carpenters, electricians, plumbers, architects – and I thought, ten years from now, twenty, thirty years from now, those men will come back here, with their kids, their grandkids, and they'll be able to point to this gym and say, "I helped build that."

That is a powerful, profound thing for any man to be able to say.

And I hope ten, twenty, thirty years from now, I hope you will come back. And you'll walk into this gym, with your kids, your grandkids, and you'll walk into that gym, and you'll look up, at the league championship banners – and there'll be more than sixteen of them – and you can look at the trophies in the trophy case – and there'll be more than three of them – and you'll be able to say, "I helped build that."

We are building something here, boys. We are building a foundation, a program, a legacy.

This is the beginning of great, great things.

All right, everybody up.

Everybody up.

One last time. No, not one last time. Because we'll all be back next year. Except for Coach Raymond. He'll be in Florida. On the beach somewhere.

So, until next November 1st.

Hands in.

And, oh, by the way. Tommy, tell em what you had for breakfast this morning.

TOMMY

Wheaties.

COACH

Wheaties! That's my boy!

> *Or "Sugar Frosted Flakes." "You did! You rascal, you! We'll have to talk about that when we get home!"*

OK, hands in.

Hands in.

And I just want to say. I have loved every minute of this season.

On three, Spartans. One, two, three …

EVERYBODY

Spartans!

Lights out.

The End

About the Author

Ed Schmidt is a playwright. The plays in this collection have been performed in his kitchen, in his dining room and living room, and in a grammar-school locker room. His other plays have been produced by the Lookingglass Theatre Company, Old Globe, Pasadena Playhouse, George Street Playhouse, Philadelphia Live Arts Festival, Bonn (Germany) Biennale, L.A. Theatre Works, Sacramento Theatre Company, Chicago Theater Company, West Bank Café, Belmont Italian-American Theatre, Ironbound Theatre, Hattiloo Theatre, and the Cornelia Street Café. He lives in Brooklyn.

www.edschmidttheater.com

About Books We Live by

Contact Information:

Books We Live by

360 West 118th Street

New York, NY 10026, USA

Visit our website BooksWeLiveby.com to find out about our publications.

###